Collecting Simpsons!
An Unofficial Guide to
Merchandise from
'The Simpsons'™

If you've ever wondered what that old Bart Simpson doll or Simpsons T-shirt is now worth to a serious collector, this is the book for you. **"Collecting Simpsons! An Unofficial Guide to Merchandise from 'The Simpsons'™,"** written by longtime Simpsons collector William LaRue, is jam-packed with descriptions and typical prices for more than 1,000 dolls, household goods, games, books, videos, posters and much, much more.

But this book isn't just one of those eye-numbing, snooze-inducing, oh-so-serious collectibles price guides. Take a look at the features inside:

■ More than 375 photos, with detailed captions.

■ A brief history of "The Simpsons" and its merchandise phenomenon.

■ Comparisons of "cool" and "cheesy" Simpsons stuff.

■ Reviews of action figures, collector plates, books, software and other goods.

■ Advice on buying animation cels.

■ An autopsy of a Bart doll (with photos).

■ A quick look at Simpsons bootlegs and promotional merchandise.

Aye, carumba! This is one "Simpsons" book that should be part of every collection.

William D. LaRue, who owns more than 3,000 items relating to "The Simpsons," is the author of the Collecting Simpsons! Web site at http://members.aol.com/bartfan. He is also the television critic for The Syracuse (N.Y.) Newspapers, and a graduate of the State University of New York at Potsdam and Syracuse University.

Collecting Simpsons!

An Unofficial Guide to Merchandise from 'The Simpsons'™

William D. LaRue

Designed by Darren A. Sanefski

Collecting Simpsons! An Unofficial Guide to Merchandise from 'The Simpsons'™

Copyright © 1999, William D. LaRue.
Library of Congress Catalog Card Number 99-73666
ISBN: 0-9675421-0-3

First printing, 1999.

U.S. residents can order additional copies of this book for $27, which includes shipping and handling. Send a check or money order, along with your mailing address, to:

KML Enterprises Publishing
Box 292
Liverpool, N.Y. 13088

For orders outside the U.S. or for more information, write the author at the above address or send e-mail to BartFan@aol.com.

Bart Simpson gingerbread cookie, 1996, The Great Australian Gingerbread Co. The cookie is about 6 by 3½ inches.

Itchy & Scratchy watch with barbershop scene, 1993, Big-Time. This watch — definitely not for the kiddies — shows Scratchy's head floating around in a bubble. Check out the back of the dial face to see a headless cat in a barber chair with Itchy, the mouse, behind him with cutting tool. One of four Itchy & Scratchy watches from Big-Time.

A display box and two wrapper variations for 16-card packs of Topps trading cards, 1990. Each pack has one "lousy" or "crummy" sticker.

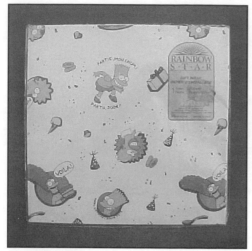

A folded sheet of Simpsons gift wrap, early 1990s, Rainbow Star. Canada. The sheet is approximately 27 by 40 inches.

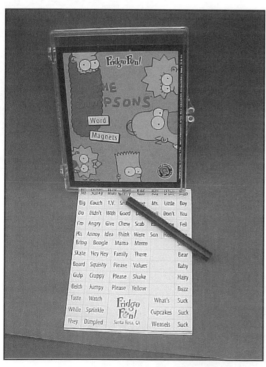

Word magnets, 1996, Fridge Fun. This unusual item consists of three magnetic vinyl sheets that can be broken into tiny rectangles to form various word combinations. There are also blank rectangles that can be filled in with a pencil.

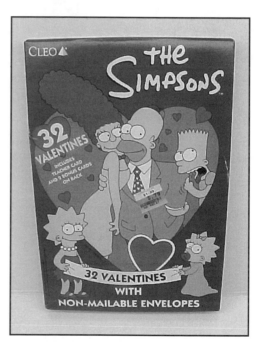

Valentine's Day boxed cards, 32-count, 1994, Cleo. Includes a teacher card and two "bonus" cards you can cut from the back of the box.

Table of contents

Introduction

....

Call of the Simpsons

Welcome to "Collecting Simpsons! An Unofficial Guide to Merchandise from The Simpsons." The fact that you're reading this brief Introduction means you're probably a fan of "The Simpsons." Or perhaps you just like self-conscious introductions to books.

In either case I hope you get a chuckle or otherwise enjoy this book. Even if you're not a collector or a fan of the animated TV series "The Simpsons," perhaps the sheer volume of fun and good-natured excesses on these pages will help to justify your having read through the entire second paragraph.

Mostly, this book is a reference guide. Here you'll find help in finding, identifying and determining typical prices for more than 1,000 Simpsons items — from dolls and action figures to compact discs and calendars. Throughout the book you'll find photos, reviews, interviews and lots of other obsessively detailed information.

Yes, this book is dedicated to the proposition that being a fan of "The Simpsons" can go way beyond the simple joy of watching one of the best shows on television. In fact, some of the fun in writing this book comes from knowing that the content will come as a shocker to many loyal viewers — lots of whom are too young to remember the huge amount of Simpsons merchandise that followed the series premiere in 1990.

But viewers of all ages can fall in love with collecting Simpsons merchandise, a passion that in recent years has enjoyed growing popularity. Although the general public's appetite for Simpsons goods faded in the early '90s, there remained a small but dedicated bunch who never lost interest. And as the years have passed, others caught on to the fun of collecting toys and other goods featuring Homer, Bart and the whole bright-yellow Simpsons gang.

A whopper of a tale

I confess. I used to think people were a bit crazy to get so wrapped up in collecting toys and other items of pop culture. It seemed a silly diversion of time and money. I wasn't even impressed when collectors justified their investment with the dubious premise it would someday put their kids through college.

My opinion didn't change even in 1990 when I bought some Simpsons dolls from Burger King, and my wife bought a Bart Simpson coin bank, doll and a key ring. We didn't plan to start a Simpsons collection. We just loved "The Simpsons" and wanted a few keepsakes.

Years passed. Then in 1995 I was digging through boxes in my basement when I pulled out the Burger King dolls and began chuckling over their strange but compelling appearance. That's when it struck me that it would be fun to

Five Simpsons plush dolls distributed by Burger King restaurants in 1990. Each comes with its own cardboard accessory. The dolls were originally sold in sealed plastic bags.

....

see if I could find other Simpsons items.

That set me off on a merchandise hunt that became such a pleasure that I launched my own Collecting Simpsons! site (http://members.aol.com/bartfan) on the World Wide Web in 1996 as a way to share the fun. As I write this, the Internet site is averaging about 350 visitors a day.

Search for private Barts

When I began to hunt for Simpsons merchandise, I thought it would be easy to put together a respectable collection. "Of course," I told myself, "I'll just head out to the mall and pick up some stuff." But to quote my talking Bart Simpson doll, "No way, man!"

I was stunned to find that, by 1995, almost all of the Simpsons merchandise had disappeared from U.S. stores. I found a few Simpsons items here and there at close-out stores, as well as flea markets and garage sales. I also ordered a few things from merchants advertising in Toy Shop magazine.

But it wasn't until I began using my personal computer to search that I was able to add to my collection on a regular basis. Through dial-up online services Prodigy, CompuServe and America Online, I soon tracked down the Pull-String Talking Bart doll, a giant Homer arcade doll, the Marge beauty bag set, and the "Simpsons Don't Have a Cow" dice game.

When I couldn't find much new through those sources, I began posting notes and reading through Internet newsgroups. This turned out to be a gold mine, providing an almost unlimited source of Simpsons merchandise from sellers and traders around the world.

3,000 items ... and growing

Today, my Simpsons collection easily tops 3,000 items, counting all of the variations, as well as promotional merchandise, magazines, home recordings

Homer Simpson 24-inch arcade doll, 1990, Acme. The company also produced an 11-inch Homer doll.

and news clippings. Thanks to a recent wave of new Simpsons merchandise in the U.K., Australia and other countries — and undoubtedly more to come in the United States — the size of my collection seems limited only by the depth of my wallet, the patience of my spouse, and the space on my storage shelves.

Indeed, I'm sometimes asked where I store all this stuff I collect. I have a few items of Simpsons merchandise displayed around the house, including posters in my two children's bedrooms

Marge Simpson Beauty Bag toy set, 1990, Mattel. Just about the only working item is the small mirror and the 6-inch-long vinyl pouch. The set also includes tiny hair rollers, as well as a pretend spray bottle labeled "Marge's hair stuff."

and a framed "Bart-O-Lounger" animation art sericel in the family room. Most items, though, are carefully stored in plastic-lined boxes on shelves to avoid damage from sunlight, moisture and variations in temperature. (I used to explain that I had everything buried in sealed vaults underground, but I stopped kidding when I realized some people actually believed me.)

The point of this guide

In writing this book, I've focused almost exclusively on licensed Simpsons merchandise — that is, goods that are approved for retail sale or distribution by Simpsons creator Matt Groening and Twentieth Century Fox Film Corp.

Which is not to say that clever bootlegs and other non-licensed items aren't worthy of interest to some collectors. I even write a bit about them here. However, there is so much legal merchandise to collect, I don't think bootlegs are worth more than a passing mention.

Almost every item listed in this book is part of my personal collection. I've also gathered information about Simpsons merchandise through conversations with other collectors and by doing lots of research on the Internet.

I have tried to be as accurate as possible in describing merchandise. But it's likely there are plenty of variations I don't know about. It's also important to note that some merchandise originally made with packaging was eventually sold at the retail level or traded without packaging — or even with totally new packaging. If I'm aware packaging exists, I've noted it. I certainly welcome corrections and suggestions from readers.

Please write to me at BartFan@aol.com. Or visit my Collecting Simpsons! Web site at http://members.aol.com/bartfan. (Wow! Two shameless plugs in the same chapter.) If you're already a Simpsons collector or plan to be one, I'd love to hear from you.

Which reminds me of an e-mail I got a couple of years ago from John Rana from Manila, Philippines. A longtime Simpsons collector, he was thrilled to discover my Web site.

"It nice to know somebody else from the other side of the galaxy collects Simpsons merchandise as well," Rana says. "May our tribe increase."

And may this book help it along.

"Deep, Deep Trouble" compact disc single, 1991, Geffen. This CD features four mixes: "Full Dance Mix," "LP Edit," "Dance Mix Edit" and "Springfield Soul Stew."

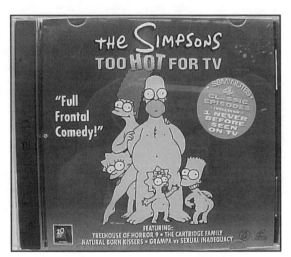

"Too Hot For TV" video compact disc, 1999, Fox Home Entertainment. Singapore and Malaysia. This two-disc VCD set (not to be confused with a DVD) can be viewed on a personal computer using Windows Media Player. It features four full-length episodes: "Treehouse of Horror 9," "The Cartridge Family," "Natural Born Kissers" and "Grampa vs. Sexual Inadequacy."

"Deep, Deep Trouble" picture disc, 1991, Geffen. This vinyl record album is shaped like Bart singing into a microphone. It features two "Deep, Deep Trouble" mixes: "Dance Mix Edit" and "LP Edit."

Acknowledgments

First, with utmost gratitude, thanks to Darren Sanefski for the cool design and layout of this book. Thanks also to Roury Williams for helpful editing suggestions; to my author-brother, Robert, for some early advice on book-publishing; to numerous Simpsons collectors, including Trina Kubeck, Robert Getz and Craig Vinton, for sharing their enthusiasm and insights over the years; and to the folks at Twentieth Century Fox Film Corp. and especially Matt Groening for bringing the world both "The Simpsons" and Simpsons merchandise.

Most of all, I thank my wonderful family, especially my wife, Kathy, who loved Simpsons merchandise even before I did; and my children, Brittany and John, who think it's pretty cool that Daddy still plays with toys.

— William D. LaRue

Chocolate shapes, 1997, St. Michael.
Canada. Set of nine milk-chocolates shaped
like Simpsons family members.

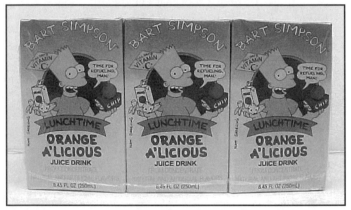

Orange A'Licious Juice Drink, 1991, Sweetripe Drinks, Canada.
This pack has three 8.45-fluid-oz. boxes of orange drink made
from concentrate.

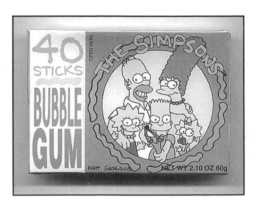

40-stick pack of Simpsons gum, 1990,
Amurol Products. The company produced a
similar pack with a design showing Bart
surfing.

1 A brief overview

Visiting with 'Bart lady'

I t's noon March 2, 1998. All across the United States, thousands of homes are tuned to a long-running national TV show devoted to antiques and collectibles. "Personal FX: The Collectibles Show" this day is visiting the Oregon home of a fan of "The Simpsons."

The camera swings toward a sofa lined with an eclectic collection of dolls: a Pull-String Talking Bart, a Homer stuffed into a box, a Lisa hanging on a card, and carefully posed Maggie and Marge.

An eternally cheerful John Davis, a field reporter for the popular collectibles show on cable network FX, is at the Portland home of Trina Kubeck, a woman whose fondness for "The Simpsons" and Simpsons collectibles prompts friends to call her "Bart Lady."

A better title might be "Simpsons super-collector." Kubeck owns about 10,000 pieces of Simpsons memorabilia, much of it displayed on shelves near the sofa.

The camera pans along the long rows of Simpsons goods — shampoo bottles, automobile air fresheners, plastic drinking cups, a water bottle, a Homer cookie jar, Franklin Mint collector plates, a desktop clock radio, a Bart-shaped chair, and an ocean of dolls. A few items are so rare that only the most dedicated Simpsons collector would even know they existed. Kubeck explains that the first Simpsons items she owned were Mattel action figures that included hilarious pop-in "word balloons" for the characters.

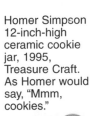

Homer Simpson 12-inch-high ceramic cookie jar, 1995, Treasure Craft. As Homer would say, "Mmm, cookies."

Simpsons 8-oz. shampoo bottles, 1991, Cosrich. A perfect item for those who want to wash those Simpsons right into their hair.

"I picked up a few pieces," she answers when Davis asks how she got started collecting Simpsons merchandise, "and before I knew it, it became an obsession for me."

Don't worry, be obsessive

Of course, obsessive behavior is nothing new for Simpsons fans. From the show's beginning, many of its viewers haven't just watched "The Simpsons." They've memorized dialogue. They've learned to imitate characters. They've debated the animated comedy's inside jokes, movie parodies and social satire.

And, like Kubeck, there are hundreds — maybe thousands — of Simpsons fans who have spent a huge chunk of cash and devoted lots of time assembling collections of merchandise featuring Bart and other characters from this hit Fox TV series.

Even Simpsons creator Matt Groening, speaking in July 1998 with

Simpsons creator Matt Groening appeared on the cover of the 11th — and final — issue of Simpsons Illustrated magazine in Summer 1993. Welsh Publishing Group created this 40-page official magazine, packed with photos, interviews and humorous features.

television critics in California, noted that he, too, enjoys Simpsons merchandise. And not just because he's made a small fortune from his cut of sales. "I like the money, but to me it's fun. I like the toys. I like doing that stuff, you know," he said. "To me, it's part of the whole experience."

A shop heard 'round the world

Over the first 10 seasons of the series, Twentieth Century Fox Film Corp., owner of "The Simpsons," has capitalized on the show's immense following by approving merchandise licenses for thousands of Simpsons items in the United States and other countries.

Without exaggeration, a collector could chew up weekly paychecks for years trying to obtain all the colors and sizes and styles of licensed Simpsons items — everything from toothbrushes to a Butterfinger candy tin to a full-size arcade pinball game from Data East. Many serious Simpsons collectors also save in-store promotional items, newspa-

Two sets of Simpsons toothbrushes, 1991, Harrison Co. Canada. One two-pack offers Bart and Lisa brushes, while the other features Homer and Marge.

per clippings, bootlegs and just about anything else relating to the show.

Despite the enormous success of "The Simpsons," it wasn't until the late 1990s that the hobby magazines and others paid much attention to fans putting together extensive collections of Simpsons merchandise.

In 1998 alone, in addition to the FX television profile, there was a cover story on Simpsons merchandise in the July issue of Toy Trader magazine. A month later Beckett Hot Toys magazine published a two-page profile of Simpsons collector Craig Vinton of Seattle. At about the same time, Simpsons collector Robert W. Getz of Warminster, Pa., authored the photo-laden book, "The Unauthorized Guide To The Simpsons Collectibles: A Handbook and Price Guide" ($29.95, Schiffer Books).

Another thing happened in 1998: Prices exploded for Simpsons merchandise on the Internet and elsewhere. On the eBay auction site on the World Wide Web, for instance, a hard-to-find Simpsons tabletop Score-O-Matic electronic pinball game sold for more than $200. That same game in 1991 sold for about $35.

Fox plans more U.S. merchandise

Just in time to respond to this renewed interest in Simpsons goods, Fox in 1998 announced plans for a juiced-up marketing strategy for products featuring Simpsons characters.

One Fox official told Variety trade magazine that the studio was making Simpsons games and other goods its "primary initiative" for licensed merchandise in the United States and other countries

Although this wave of new merchandise has been slow in coming in the U.S., the plan still sounds smart. Fox has enjoyed great success in recent years rolling out Simpsons merchandise in the U.K. and Australia. This includes apparel, clothing accessories, gifts and novelty items, stationery, housewares, sporting goods, food and published materials.

Well, maybe you should worry

Of course, lots of wonderful new merchandise might create more "war stories" like this one Kubeck revealed to "Personal FX":

Our favorite lines

For a Simpsons collector, even the subtlest of references on "The Simpsons" to toys, collectibles and other merchandise are treasures in themselves.

Here are a few:

■ "How can you love a box or a toy or graphics? You're a grown man!" (Homer Simpson, in "Homer Phobia.")

■ "I'd be mortified if someone ever made a lousy product with the Simpson name on it." (Lisa Simpson, in "Lisa Vs. Malibu Stacy.")

■ "Are those the limited-edition action figures?" (Principal Skinner, in "Lisa's Rival.")

■ "Fifty bucks for a toy? No kid is worth that!" (Homer Simpson, in "Homer Phobia.")

■ "I'd never lend my name to an inferior product." (Bart Simpson, in "Kamp Krusty.")

One day in the early 1990s she spotted the gorgeous but elusive Score-O-Matic toy pinball machine out of reach on a top shelf at Kmart.

"I tried to climb the shelf," Kubeck recalled. "I saw the colors. I couldn't get to it. So I had to ring the flashing red lights and scream and holler until they came running. I told them I'd just tear down the store if they didn't get it for me quickly."

Kubeck got her machine, a piece of merchandise so fun that even FX reporter Davis couldn't resist a quick shot or two.

Simpsons Score-O-Matic battery-operated desktop pinball, 1990, Sharon Industries. 20-inch-long metal and plastic game. Counter rotates with each point scored with the metal pinball. Uses four C batteries, not included.

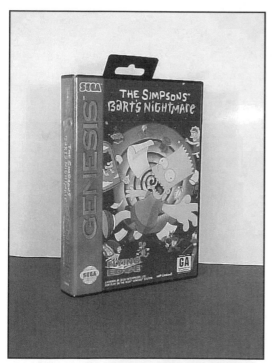

"Bart's Nightmare" Sega Genesis game, 1993, Flying Edge. Packaging reads: "Eight levels, each one scarier than the last, with villains like Homer Kong, Momthra, and Barney Gumble riding a pink elephant."

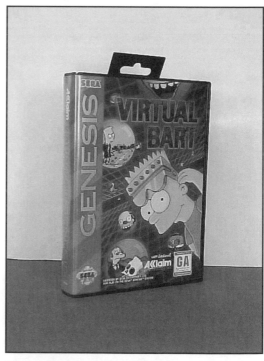

"Virtual Bart" Sega Genesis game, 1993, Acclaim. Packaging reads: "Bart's in a heap of technical trouble — he's stuck in a virtual reality machine!!! Enter the Jurassic era as Dino Bart, and stomp through stone age mayhem."

Book review

In the introduction to **"The Simpsons: A Complete Guide to Our Favorite Family,"** series creator Matt Groening writes that this isn't just another one of those "cheapo, cash-in, whip-it-out, crummy guides." He isn't kidding.

"A Complete Guide" ($15.95 soft cover, $25 hard cover, Harper Perennial, 1997 & 1998) is cleverly written. It's got a sense of humor. It's beautifully designed. The book even features screen shots from the series, as well as lots of original art.

Each chapter of this 249-page publication is devoted to a single season, with at least one page for each episode. The detail is staggering. For each episode, you get a plot summary, the original air date, the name of the writer and director, and snippets of dialogue. There are also chalkboard sayings for every episode in which one appeared.

One of the best features in the book is "The Stuff You May Have Missed," which summarizes some of the half-hidden gags that viewers might have overlooked if they didn't freeze the tape. An added treat are tongue-in-cheek biographies of Simpsons characters, from Llewellyn Sinclair to The Comic Book Guy.

Stuffed between the episode summaries are a variety of in-depth lists, including a guide to every appearance of Itchy & Scratchy and a summary of the fictional Krusty the Clown merchandise on the show. (Wouldn't you just love to own a Krusty Jack-in-the-Box?)

2 'The Simpsons'

A landmark TV comedy

To understand the popularity of Simpsons merchandise, you have to understand why "The Simpsons" TV series became a hit.

In one episode Homer Simpson tells his wife, Marge, that he finds it hard to fake interest in her "kooky" projects.

Marge: "What kooky projects?"

Homer: "You know, the painting class, the first-aid course, the whole Lamaze thing."

Can you imagine writers on "The Flintstones" — or for recent hit "South Park" — coming up with something so smartly funny as that?

"The Simpsons" has all the key elements of a great TV series — memorable characters, sharp writing and good performances.

Unlike its many imitators, "The Simpsons" is already a classic TV comedy, a critically acclaimed cartoon for grown-ups that skillfully blends parody, topical themes and surreal situations. The writers even manage to squeeze in some unabashed sentiment, although rarely does it go overboard.

And unlike many comedies that lower their standards to win lots of viewers, "The Simpsons" is also a hit with tough TV critics.

In 1993 Entertainment Weekly called "The Simpsons" a series that puts "other comedies to shame."

The magazine added:

Simpsons trading cards from Topps, 1990. Trading cards of older-style phased out by most manufacturers in the early 1990s. One side features a screen shot from a TV episode (often early Simpsons shorts from "The Tracey Ullman Show.") The other side has a trivia quiz. Pictured here are two cards from the U.S. version, and one card from a similar set distributed in Germany.

People have been investing strong emotions in cartoon characters at least as far back as Mickey Mouse; the sustained cleverness and, yes, humanity of "The Simpsons" proves that our devotion is not misplaced.

'Tracey'-ing the show's roots

Let's flash back in time to the somewhat humble beginnings of "The Simpsons." The show's characters first appeared in 1987 as cartoon snippets airing between sketches on Fox television's comedy series "The Tracey Ullman Show."

The creator of these comic shorts was Matt Groening, then a successful but little-known counterculture cartoonist.

His "Life in Hell" comic strip, featuring bug-eyed rabbits, appeared in many alternative and college newspapers.

Invited to create an animated version for the "Ullman" show, Groening — fearful of losing rights to his rabbits — instead sketched a family of bug-eyed, crudely drawn humans he called the Simpsons.

These early Simpsons cartoons on "Tracey Ullman" quickly set the tone for the smart, irreverent humor that would became the show's trademark.

The first Simpsons short featured Homer and Marge Simpson inadvertently terrorizing their three young children, Bart, Lisa and Maggie, with traditional bedtime banter about bed bugs and cradles falling out of tree tops.

Over the next two years, as the Simpsons emerged as clearly defined characters, "Tracey Ullman" producer James L. Brooks convinced skeptical Fox executives that these shorts would make a great full-fledged TV series.

"The Simpsons Christmas Special" home video, 1991, Fox Video. VHS cassette of the first Simpsons Christmas special from 1989.

A Simpsons Christmas present

The first half-hour episode of "The Simpsons" aired in December 1989 as a Christmas special, "Simpsons Roasting on an Open Fire." It's now available on home video as "The Simpsons Christmas Special" ($9.98, Fox Video).

In this episode, Homer gets a job as a department store Santa so he can afford to buy presents for his family. Marge can't chip in because she's spent her Christmas savings to get a tattoo removed from Bart's arm. Homer eventually blows his $13 Santa salary by betting on a pathetic mutt at the dog track.

All is not lost, though. Homer finds the perfect Christmas present by agreeing to let Bart adopt the dog. But just as the holiday sentimentality seems ready to overtake the Simpsons clan, the family provides a violent rendition of "Rudolph, the Red-Nosed Reindeer" over closing credits that returns the show to its edgy roots.

"The Simpsons" premiered as a series Jan. 14, 1990, with the hilarious episode "Bart the Genius." Ten-year-old Bart is mistakenly sent to a school for gifted children after he switches his aptitude test with another student. As with the Christmas episode, Bart shows almost no respect for authority figures, including his hapless father. Bart calls him "a big, dumb, balding North American ape."

The show's ratings exploded. Within two months, "The Simpsons" became one of the top 15 most-watched American shows — a spectacular feat for the Fox television network, which then was still unavailable to 20 percent of the U.S.

Meet those wacky Simpsons

Matt Groening conceived "The Simpsons" as the world's most dysfunctional family, headed by doltish Homer Simpson. A man with the charm of a loud belch, he once gave Marge a bowling ball as a birthday present — inscribed with his own name.

Marge is a loving wife whose life revolves around running the household, getting the kids off to school and bailing Homer out of trouble. Marge has a mind of her own, though, displayed prominently in the first-season episode "Itchy & Scratchy & Marge," where she embarks on a campaign to rid television cartoons of violence.

Mischief-maker Bart is a modern-day Dennis the Menace, except Bart knows a lot more cuss words. When he's not telling some adult to "Eat my shorts!" — a saying that would often appear on early Simpsons merchandise — Bart is spray-painting his name on a school building or stealing a car to take friends on a trip to Tennessee.

Lisa, 8, is the brainiest of the bunch, a saxophone-playing second-grader who laments that Bart's antics make him popular with other kids. Some of the most thoughtful episodes of "The Simpsons" have centered on Lisa.

Youngest child Maggie does little except suck on her pacifier. She's barely uttered a word in all these years, but don't take her lightly. She's the one who pulled the trigger in the famous "Who Shot Mr. Burns?" two-part cliffhanger that was a collector's dream for its unusual amount of promotional merchandise.

Some fans have favorite characters who are part of the supporting cast, which includes grouchy kid-show host Krusty the Clown, do-good neighbor Ned Flanders, nasty nuclear-plant owner Montgomery Burns, his (barely) closeted gay assistant Waylon Smithers, and Marge's crabby sisters Patty and Selma, whom Homer nicknamed "the gruesome twosome."

Freeze-frame jokes

More than just zany characters, "The Simpsons" zips along with lots of sight gags and other surprises which often speed by so quickly that many fans use the freeze-frame buttons on their video players to catch them.

A typical episode contains background signs and other visual gags that the writers slip half-hidden into each episode, such as the Squishy ice-drink machine at the Kwik-E-Mart, where settings included one labeled "Experimental."

Such background gags helped to inspire the official 1997 book "The Simpsons: A Complete Guide to Our Family" ($14.95 soft cover, $25 hard cover, Harper Collins). The guide, which Groening helped edit, contains summaries of each episode, including lists of those freeze-frame jokes.

"I love that," Groening has said of these gags. "I love the idea that we put in jokes that kids don't get. And that later, when they grow up, and they read a few books, and go to college, and watch the show again, they can get the show on a completely different level."

"The Simpsons" definitely rewards careful viewing. Film buffs often chuckle over obscure references to "Citizen Kane" and "Thelma & Louise." Couch potatoes will make a fuss over references to classic shows such as "The Twilight Zone" and "M*A*S*H."

Much like devotees of "Star Trek," many Simpsons fans are almost cult-like in their dedication to memorizing dialogue and their devotion to the actors. By early 1999, there were more than 1,000 fan sites on the Internet focusing on "The Simpsons."

No one as of late 1999 had organized a full-fledged official "Simpsons" convention, but lots of fans are definitely enthusiastic that the show has lived long and prospered.

"They (Simpsons fans) really go berserk," said actress Yeardley Smith, the voice of Lisa, in a 1996 interview. "They know the details. They'll go, 'You remember the episode where blah, blah, blah.' And you think, no, I don't. That was eight months ago for me, or longer."

Although "The Simpsons" doesn't enjoy the huge TV viewership of the biggest hits such as "ER" and "60 Minutes," it's been a lasting winner in other ways that ensure it will be around for a long time. The show remains among the top programs with viewers ages 18 to 34, the demographic group advertisers most want to reach. In commercial TV, especially on Fox, that's the only measurement that truly counts.

'The dumbest thing'

Despite the critical acclaim and high ratings, not everyone has fallen in love with "The Simpsons." That was especially true in the show's early days when many Americans were still getting used to a cartoon with a foul-mouthed kid, a battling family, and lots of jabs at politicians, entertainers, corporate titans and others.

First Lady Barbara Bush called the show "the dumbest thing I've ever seen." Nuclear power executives complained that Springfield's leaking nuclear plant — which causes fish in a nearby lake to have three eyes — was unfairly giving their industry a black eye. And many schools banned Bart Simpson T-shirts, including ones carrying a line from the show, "I'm Bart Simpson. Who the hell are you?"

It was only after television gave birth in the mid-1990s to cartoons with darker, more threatening themes — shows like "Beavis and Butt-head" and "South Park" — that objections over "The Simpsons" all but disappeared.

"It's amazing that behavior once considered outrageous isn't so outrageous anymore," then-executive producer Bill Oakley said in a 1996 interview with the Seattle Times. "You can now hear profanity at 10 p.m., so hearing Bart say 'Eat my shorts' or talk back to his teacher isn't so shocking today. I guess America has changed around 'The Simpsons.'"

The show's legacy

No one at the Fox network is talking about pulling the plug on "The Simpsons" anytime soon.

But even if new episodes ceased right away, "The Simpsons" has ensured itself the status of a TV classic, according to Syracuse University broadcasting professor Robert Thompson, director of the Center for the Study of Popular Television.

"Twenty years from now, 'The Simpsons' will be much more remembered than 'ER' ever will be," Thompson says. "In terms of writing, I would say 'The Simpsons' is one of the top five of all time."

For a while, Simpsons merchandise was also a huge hit in America. But enduring on TV turned out to be a lot easier than ruling the toy shelves.

Lisa Simpson Action Wind Up figure, 1990,
Mattel. 3-inch-high figure on a small wind-up car.

Bart Simpson Valentine vinyl doll, 1990, Dan
Dee. 12 inches high with red kiss marks on his
face. His pink shirt says, "Cooties, man!"

Lisa Simpson bean bag doll,
1993, Jemini. France. 6 inches
high with vinyl head and bean-bag
body.

Bart Simpson "Eat my shorts, man!"
framed poster, 1990, Western
Graphics Corp. 20-by-15-inch.

Bart Simpson "I'm Bart Simpson. Who
the hell are you?" framed poster,
1990, Can-Am Global Trading Co.
Canada. 20-by-15-inch.

Bart Simpson "Underachiever" poster, 1990,
Western Graphics Corp. 20-by-15-inch. This
poster was sometimes sold framed.

3 A history: Boom, bust and Bart

Bart, Bart everywhere

At state fairs across the country in the summer of 1990, nothing was hotter than Bart Simpson. Fairgoers couldn't step on the midway without seeing row upon row of Bart dolls hanging from one booth after another like so many pieces of yellow meat.

These 24-inch furry arcade dolls from Acme were soon followed in America by Simpsons dolls that Burger King restaurants distributed in a hugely popular promotion.

Simpsons merchandise also took a big bite of retail shelf space. Shoppers were enticed at the mall, supermarket and drug store with shelves and racks that nearly sagged with Simpsons dolls, figures, bumper stickers, automobile window hangers, posters, water bottles, hats, buttons, towels and T-shirts.

In fact, more than any other product, T-shirts defined the early Simpsons merchandising boom. Buyers snapped up shirts featuring

Simpsons 1½-inch-diameter buttons, 1989 and 1990, Button-Up.

Simpsons "Mystery of Life" board game, 1990, Cardinal. The object is to be the first player to make it home after getting all five items on an "agenda card" checked off. There's also a "deluxe" version with PVC figures, instead of cardboard game pieces.

"The Simpsons" so fast that some merchants hawked them right out of packing boxes. One report estimated that the shirts were selling for a while at the stunning rate of 1 million a week.

"There was a public demand, practically an outcry, for Simpsons products," wrote Steve Dale and Shane Tritsch in their unofficial 1990 book, "Simpson Mania," from Consumer Guide.

Schoolchildren returned to classes in fall 1990 with Simpsons backpacks, notebooks, pencils and lunch boxes.

But many kids learned a lesson in political correctness when they dared wear a favorite Bart shirt that announced: "Underachiever ... and proud of it!" Many principals and school boards banned this shirt and other Simpsons clothing, arguing that Bart was a poor role model. Because of the outcry, J.C. Penney even halted sales of the "Underachiever" shirt.

Still, Christmas 1990 was huge for Simpsons merchandise. Stores sold almost everything imaginable in the Simpsons line, from Jesco's bendable action figures to Cardinal's "Mystery of Life" board game.

Playthings, a toy-trade magazine, summed up the early holiday retail season of 1990 this way: "Anything in the Simpsons line rated well."

27

$750 million in sales in 1990

Simpsons merchandise in 1990 chalked up an estimated $750 million in retail sales. Products from the show placed third in U.S. sales, not far behind "Teenage Mutant Ninja Turtles," according to Licensing Letter, an industry newsletter.

In the first full season of "The Simpsons," Twentieth Century Fox reportedly signed more than 100 U.S. licensing agreements for the show. In other countries, the availability of Simpsons merchandise was also widespread. In Japan alone, Fox was said to have sold $30 million in licensed Simpsons merchandise in 1991 — and that's before the show went on the air there.

"Really Rude" Bart Simpson doll, 1990, Mattel. Squeeze his belly and this 12-inch Bart makes flatulence sounds.

Certainly not every hit TV show spawns so many goods. So why was there so much Simpsons merchandise?

Credit the unusual, ugly-but-cute appearance of the Simpsons for fueling much of the sales. Unlike lovable cartoon characters of the past, the Simpsons taunted mainstream public sensibilities with their spiked hair, bright-yellow skin, bulging eyeballs and bad overbites.

Kids loved the merchandise's wacky appearance; teens wallowed in the rebellious spirit it represented; Baby Boomers thought the stuff was a great novelty.

One other factor led to so much merchandise: Fox saw "The Simpsons" as a huge cash cow. Rather than limit Simpsons merchandise to a few high-quality items, the studio sold merchandise licenses to just about any manufacturer who could pay the fees.

Trading cards and a talking doll

Simpsons creator Matt Groening once explained his role in the huge success of Simpsons merchandise by joking, "I don't control the tidal wave of 'Simpsons' success, but I try to surf on it as best I can."

That deep ocean of Simpsons merchandise turned out to be home to some pretty fine catches.

Among the best was a series of action figures from Mattel with their own attachable word balloons. Mattel also created a great set of Simpsons dolls, including a "Really Rude" Bart that makes flatulence noises.

Also popular with fans is Dan Dee's Pull-String Talking Bart doll, which features six "smart-aleck" sayings including, "Kids in TV land, you're being duped!"

On the other hand, too many companies capitalized on the popularity of "The Simpsons" by producing some cheaply made goods, such as trading cards from Topps that feature uninspired, blurry images.

Other manufacturers turned out products that were little more than cheap generic goods with slapped-on likenesses of Bart Simpson and other characters spouting tired catch phrases, such as Bart's "Don't have a cow, man!" or "Aye, carumba!"

Groening — whose office is decorated with mugs, books and other Simpsons goods — has acknowledged that the merchandising overkill was a bit "obnoxious."

"But I think people tend to reconcile themselves to all the bumper stickers and hanging air fresheners because the show is so clever and so good," Groening told the Los Angeles Daily News in 1993.

Bootlegs ride Simpsons success

A fan can usually tell if a Simpsons item is licensed by looking for Groening's stamped-on signature, as well as the Twentieth Century Fox Film Corp. copyright, sometimes abbreviated TCFFC.

Such markings are important because "The Simpsons" sparked lots of counterfeit merchandise, especially in the show's earliest days.

Some bootlegs are so ugly that a few uninformed (or unscrupulous) sellers have claimed they are licensed toys modeled after the crudely drawn Simpsons that first appeared in the 1980s as shorts on "The Tracey Ullman Show." Another popular claim is that these sour-faced bootlegs are "evil" versions of the Simpsons characters.

Because some bootlegs have a certain brazen charm, Simpsons fans often sneak a few into their collections. Some knockoffs are cool enough to impress even Groening, who has made room in his office for a bootleg plaster bust of Bart wearing a sombrero. "I've always said that copyright infringement is the ultimate compliment," he once said.

Even so, Twentieth Century Fox attorneys continue to target flagrant bootleggers in order to protect the company's rights to the characters.

Not long ago, Fox successfully sued an Australian firm that briefly distributed its own Duff Beer, which featured a packaging clearly inspired by Homer's fictitious favorite brand. Since then, some industrious Australians who bought up cases of the stuff are selling unlicensed Duff for about $45 a can on the Internet.

No licensed beer or cereal

Long before this beer case in Australia, Groening and Fox turned down a pitch for a licensed Duff. "We had some legitimate requests to put out the beer, but that's something I said we absolutely shouldn't do. I wasn't going to have 'The Simpsons' encouraging kids to drink alcohol," Groening told The Los Angeles Times.

Sometimes, though, rejection works the other way. Groening revealed that food makers turned down his proposal for a Simpsons cereal, one that would be a parody of highly sugared ones. He wanted a vibrantly colored box to attract children — except his cereal actually would have some nutritional value.

"A sugarless cereal — just my idea for a small public service to the kids of America," Groening said wistfully. "But we couldn't get one cereal company to go along with the idea of a healthy cereal for kids. I said, 'How about a low-sugar cereal?' Nope, not good enough."

Oversaturation of merchandise

Despite the show's continued popularity, U.S. sales for Simpsons merchandise by 1992 had drooped lower than a Charles Montgomery Burns smile. In 1990, "The Simpsons" recorded about $750 million in domestic sales. Two years later, sales dwindled to a reported $225 million and to a relative trickle after that.

This drop didn't surprise experts. A swift decline in sales is typical for the character-related licensing business.

However, the decline in sales for Simpsons merchandise is also seen as the result of tremendous overproduction.

"Simpsons characters have just absolutely died," a spokesman for Cub Foods told Supermarket News in February 1991. "We had a supply of Simpsons dolls left over from the Christmas selling season, and from all indications that license has passed its peak. If we get into it on back-to-school products, we may not go too deeply with the character. It will depend on the item."

The sad state of merchandise

By 1995, Simpsons merchandise had all but disappeared from shelves at Toys 'R' Us, Kmart and other retail stores in the U.S. What was left was little more than trading cards, T-shirts, a compact disc, a computer screensaver, comic books and cookie jars.

Efforts by Fox in 1993 and 1994 to revive U.S. interest in Simpsons merchandise with home furnishings mostly failed.

The studio has had more success recently overseas, where in the late 1990s it issued hundreds of licenses for Simpsons dolls, action figures, mugs and other merchandise in the United Kingdom, Australia and elsewhere.

Fox in 1998 announced plans to revive its U.S. line of Simpsons merchandise. But no one expects a return to past excesses that even inspired a brutal inside joke in the episode "Lisa vs. Malibu Stacy." In it Lisa proclaims, "I'd be mortified if someone ever made a lousy product with the Simpson name on it."

Clip-on Bart Simpson figure, 1990, Dan Dee. 5-inch-high vinyl with arms that grasp. Packaging reads: "I clip anywhere, dude!"

Bart Simpson Hang Arounds wind sock, Bart, 1990, Spectra Star. 14-inch hollow cloth made of 100 percent nylon. Box suggests these places for hanging Bart: the car, the yard, a bicycle's handle bar, on door knobs in the house.

Bart Simpson 16-inch rag doll, 1990, Dan Dee. All-cloth with large plastic eyes. Box shows Bart on skateboard saying, "Whoa Mama!"

Homer Simpson milk chocolate egg, 1998, Waikato Valley Chocolates. Australia. 120-gram, egg-shaped chocolate wrapped in yellow foil. The "Homer surprise" inside is a Krusty the Clown ball-point pen.

Bart Simpson milk chocolate egg, 1998, Waikato Valley Chocolates. Australia. 70-gram, egg-shaped chocolate wrapped in red foil. The "special Bart surprise" inside is a Bart ball-point pen.

Marge Simpson "Born to cook" chocolate egg, 1998, Waikato Valley Chocolates. 70-gram, egg-shaped chocolate wrapped in green foil. Box features instructions for cutting out the Lisa and Maggie characters from the side of the box to make standup figures.

4 Bootlegs: Fake Simpsons

A bootleg "Air Simpson" T-shirt from 1990. Other unauthorized Simpsons shirts that year included "Rasta Bart," "Teenage Mutant Ninja Simpson," "Mr. Bart Simpson for President" and "M.C. Bart."

Two crude bootleg Bart

Simpson dolls, each about 10 inches high, sometimes billed as "evil" versions of the Simpson boy.

Bootlegs are so strongly associated with "The Simpsons" that it's hard to write about Simpsons merchandise without talking about them.

But a bootleg isn't simply unlicensed merchandise, such as magazine covers or even an unauthorized collectibles book such as this. Bootlegs are items manufactured to fool the public into thinking they are licensed goods, although they were never authorized for public distribution by Twentieth Century Fox or its licensees.

The most famous of Simpsons bootlegs are cans of Duff Beer with a design clearly inspired by Homer Simpson's favorite fictional brew. Duff Beer was produced briefly by an Australian company before Twentieth Century Fox's lawyers won a court order in 1996 to stop production.

The huge early demand for Simpsons T-shirts also sparked bootlegs, including ones featuring a "Black Bart." One of the best-known is kind of a double bootleg: Bart Simpson dressed as basketball star Michael Jordan under the caption "Air Simpson."

Bootleg

Simpsons dolls also appeared with features so distorted that it's hard to imagine anyone mistaking them for the real thing. Don't believe claims these are based on early drawings of the Simpsons before the animation started getting good.

Equally ugly are several hollow plastic Simpsons key rings we found in Canada in 1996. Maggie's features are so bloated on one key ring that she's almost unrecognizable. Also in this category of bootleg weirdness is one tiny car-window pillow we found with a crudely drawn Bartman dressed as Santa.

Ceramic bootleg marionettes of Marge and Bart Simpson sold in the Czech Republic in the mid-1990s. Actually one of the better knock-offs, there is fine detail on the heads, as well as an intricate puppet mechanism.

A bit more convincing are some finely made ceramic marionettes sold in the Czech Republic in the mid-1990s. Although clothing on the Bart and Marge marionettes we tracked down isn't like anything we've seen the characters wear,

the rest of the puppets are almost credible.

Some bootlegs are simply hilarious for their sheer chutzpah. That's certainly the case with one bootleg from the Czech Republic showing a skateboarding Bart Simpson. The features are slightly distorted and the box calls him "Fancy Boy," but with its yellow skin, spiky hair and massive overbite, there's no mistaking this for anything but a Bart bootleg.

Bartman pillow, about 5 inches high, with suction cup on top for hanging it from a window.

Bootleg hollow-plastic Simpsons key rings, which we picked up for $1.99 each at a shop in Canada. Marge is about 3 inches high.

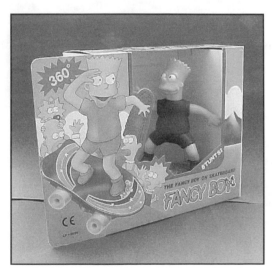

He's billed on the display box as "Fancy Boy," but this skateboarding figure is clearly a Bart Simpson bootleg found in the Czech Republic. Note the packaging shows oddly drawn variations of the Simpsons family members.

5 Promos: Not for retail

5½-inch-high glass Duff beer mug, a promotional item distributed in 1993. The other side notes the 100th episode of "The Simpsons."

Letterman-style crew jacket, early 1990s from East West, distributed to cast and crew on "The Simpsons." Black and red coat, with stitched-on patches.

Not all official Simpsons merchandise is sold in retail stores. Fox also gives away a lot of promotional goods, or "promos," to employees, TV and radio stations, and others to publicize the TV series. The relative rarity and often-cool inventiveness of these promos make them highly desired by Simpsons collectors.

T-shirts are a frequently issued type of promo. For its May 1996 "Homerpalooza" episode, for instance, the Fox network issued a memorable T-shirt showing Homer crooning into a microphone. Around him, with fingers stuck in their ears, are cartoon versions of rockers Peter Frampton, The Smashing Pumpkins, Cypress Hill and Sonic Youth.

Another promo shirt features the 3-D Homer from the Halloween 1995 episode. The caption on the shirt quotes Homer's inside joke in the episode about the high-price 3-D special effects. "Man," this T-shirt says, "this place looks expensive!"

Fox also released a shirt in 1997 to mark the occasion when "The Simpsons" passed "The Flintstones" as the longest-running

T-shirt features the 3-D Homer Simpson from the Halloween 1995 episode. He's saying, "Man, this place looks expensive!"

prime-time animated TV series in history. The T-shirt shows the Simpsons dressed in a parody of Fred, Wilma and the rest of the prehistoric gang.

Another promo shirt displays a line-up of about 40 of the most popular characters on the show, from Professor Frink to Waylon Smithers.

Promotional variation of Rhino Records' 1997 album, "Songs in the Key of Springfield." This one features hilarious message from loser actor Troy McClure.

T-shirt from Fox for its May 1996 "Homerpalooza" episode. Homer Simpson is surrounded by rock stars Peter Frampton, The Smashing Pumpkins, Cypress Hill and Sonic Youth.

Some other memorable Simpsons promotional items include:

■ A tiny, clear-plastic desk clock for the 200th episode in 1998. A balloon sweeps around the dial to count off the seconds.

■ A heavy-duty glass Duff beer mug showing Barney, Springfield's resident drunk, saying, "I can't get enough of that wonderful Duff."

■ A variation of Rhino Records' 1997 album, "Songs in the Key of Springfield." This one features a cardboard sleeve with a hilarious message from smiling announcer Troy McClure, who tells readers that this package "will not only enhance your CD collection but also tighten those abs with almost no dieting or exercise." Geffen Records also released numerous promotional compact discs for its 1991 album, "The Simpsons Sing the Blues," but none comes close to being as clever as the Rhino one.

■ A framed, 9-by-12-inch plaque designed to look like a gold record for the song "Baby on Board" from the fifth-season episode, "Homer's Barbershop Quartet." The details on this promo are astounding, including a fake replica of The Be Sharps' album cover. The inscription reads: "Presented to THE BE SHARPS in recognition of the musical contribution this 'Fab Four' has made with their hit BABY ON BOARD (which has sold a whole bunch of records)".

Promotional shirt displays a replica of a patch created for a 1997 research project by the University of Kansas Medical Center, which unleashed a payload of sea urchin sperm on two Atlantis shuttle flights.

Clear plastic Simpsons desk clock, just 2½ inches high, from Fox promoting its 200th episode in 1998. The sweep second hand is in the shape of a balloon that moves around the dial seemingly unsupported by anything.

A framed plaque with a mock gold record for the song "Baby on Board" from the fifth-season episode, "Homer's Barbershop Quartet," in 1993.

6 Cool vs. cheesy

The good, the bad and the downright smelly

A few years ago Simpsons creator Matt Groening gushed about a chess set with pieces shaped like Grampa, Homer, Marge and the Simpson children.

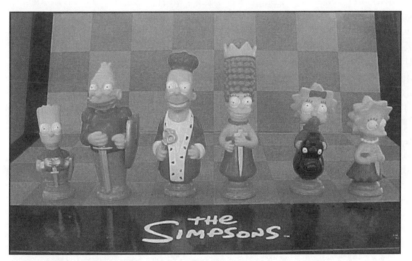

Simpsons 3-D Chess Set, 1991, Wood Expressions. Plastic chess pieces shaped like Bart (pawn), Marge (queen), Lisa (bishop), Homer (king), Maggie (horse) and Grampa (knight).

"I got very excited about the Simpsons chess set, brought one home, and my kids have learned to play chess as a result," he told The Los Angeles Times in 1997. "So I can say that the licensing of 'The Simpsons' has done at least one bit of good that I know of."

Truth be told, licensing of Simpsons merchandise also produced lots of good laughs at the expense of Groening & Co. Even Mad magazine poked fun at the seeming willingness of Twentieth Century Fox to slap a Simpson face on just about any product.

In one parody, Mad offered a "peek behind the scenes at 'The Simpsons' studio" where two employees in the product department show off some of the latest merchandise.

"Look, Friedman, I know that so far every shoddy 'Simpsons' product we've come up with sold millions, but do you really think people will buy a Marge Simpson Clogged Drain Snake?" one said as he held up the tall plumbing tool shaped like Marge.

"Sure they will!" another employee replied. "Look how well we've done with our latest product: The Bart Simpson Head Grocery Bag!"

The sad truth is that both of these fanciful products aren't a huge stretch from some of the cheesy Simpsons items that did appear on the market.

Some were so bad, in fact, that they quickly sunk into obscurity, making them hard-to-find collectibles.

Fortunately, for each Simpsons merchandise sinner there was usually a winner in the same category. We've put together a few examples:

Action figures

Cool: Mattel — they're swell

One doesn't need to be a connoisseur of toys to see right away that Mattel's Simpsons action figures are must-have toys for any serious collector. Even if you think typical prices of $25 or more for these out-of-production figures are excessive, it's hard to dispute that they are super-looking toys. (Photos on pages 43 and 44.)

Action figures of all kinds are certainly among the hottest toys on the market. They've grown steadily in popularity over the years, beginning in 1964 when G.I. Joe made its debut. This was the first "action figure" with moving parts, essentially a "doll" for boys.

With its colorful characters, "The Simpsons" is well-suited for a creative line of action figures. Indeed, Mattel's posable figures from 1990 are clever and well-made, with "word balloon" accessories capturing the spirit of the show. Including a figure of bully Nelson was a nice touch, giving children an evil foe if they actually want to play with the toys. Even the packaging on these figures is better, with boxy clear plastic that offers the look of a miniature display case.

Cheesy: Jesco bendables

Who would want to display Simpsons bendable figures from Jesco? The best thing that can be said about the rubber-like figures from 1990 is that they're durable — although maybe a bit too durable, as Homer comes off like a big rubber lump.

The figures are solid in detail but lack any Simpsons-esque cleverness. There is nothing truly memorable about them, except for Homer's overwhelming girth.

Bart Simpson Bendable Action Figure, 1990, Jesco. The rubber-like figure stands about 4½ inches high.

Dolls

Cool: Pull-String Talking Bart

The mouthy Pull-String Talking Bart Simpson doll from Dan Dee Imports is always a conversation-starter.

Pull the cord on this 18-inch vinyl and cloth doll and listen to some of these "smart-aleck" sayings:

Pull ... "Don't have a cow, man!"
Pull ... "Au contraire, mon frere!"
Pull ... "Kids in TV land, you're being duped!"

It's great when Simpsons merchandise does such a good job of reflecting the tone of a character. One sour note: The voice boxes on many of these 1990 dolls talk too fast. Many owners have to slightly grasp the pull string when they release it in order to get the doll to stop sounding like Porky Pig.

Cheesy: Burger King dolls

Perhaps the best-known Simpsons dolls — and perhaps the ugliest — are a promotional set from Burger King restaurants that were sold in fall 1990. These dolls remain popular with collectors, although their widespread distribution and somewhat distorted features make them worth far less than many of their owners imagine.

Even Yeardley Smith, the voice of Lisa Simpson, had nothing good to say about them. "It was like, 'What happened to these poor little characters? They went into the meat grinder,'" she said of the Burger King dolls in a 1996 interview.

Games

Pull-String Talking Bart Simpson doll, 1990, Dan Dee. The "Whoa mama!" printed on the shirt is one of several variations for this doll.

Cool: Arcade pinball machine

Looking for the ultimate Simpsons collectible? Toss away some of that boring antique furniture and make room in your home for the mother of all Simpsons electronic collectibles — the full-size arcade pinball game.

The game from Data East has won raves for its play and design. Bounce around cooling towers to increase the "nuclear power value." Knock down Principal Skinner, Mr. Burns, Nelson and others to light the

"The Simpsons: A Complete Guide to Our Favorite Family," 1997, HarperPerennial. This guide to Simpsons episodes sold more than 400,000 copies in its first year.

Cool: 'Complete Guide'

No Simpsons book to date has generated more sales than "A Complete Guide to Our Favorite Family" from HarperPerennial. Each chapter focuses on a single season of "The Simpsons," with at least one page for each episode. For each, you get a plot summary, the original air date, the name of the writer and director, and snippets of dialogue. There is also the full text of Bart's writing on the chalkboard in the opening credits.

The book helps squeeze even more fun out of every episode.

Cheesy: 'Simpson Fever!'

This 1990 paperback by Jeff Rovin and published by St. Martin's Paperbacks is an unofficial Simpsons fact and quiz book. At 115 pages, with no pictures and barely any sense of humor, this is one only for collectors who insist on owning everything.

Bonus Hold. Hear real voices of Homer, Bart, Apu, Krusty the Clown and others as you rack up points.

The clever faithfulness to "The Simpsons" is partly the work of Groening, who told the Los Angeles Daily News in 1993 that he had a hand in the design. "(T)he success of 'The Simpsons' has allowed me to do all the goofy stuff I always wanted to as a kid. Like design a pinball machine. My little doodles are all over the machine. Who else can say that?"

Cheesy: Homer Simpson Pop-Gun Target Set

This 1990 children's game from Ja-Ru features hollow plastic shaped like a gun that you squeeze to fire two balls at two Homer targets. Printed on the back of the package are safety rules: "A. Do not point at people or animals. B. Do not attempt to shoot any object except those especially designed balls. C. When not in use, make sure not loaded. D. Always have adult supervision while shooting."

Only a moron — or someone with a sharp sense of irony — could conceive of something as dopey as a cheap plastic gun that can only shoot about a foot but has more safety advice than an NRA shooting range.

"Simpson Fever!" 1990, St. Martin's Paperbacks. By Jeff Rovin. A 115-page unofficial guide featuring trivia quizzes and "fast facts."

Household goods

Cool: Bart and Homer cookie jars

Bart Simpson cookie jar, 1995, Treasure Craft. The company also produced a Homer Simpson cookie jar.

Outstanding in design are Treasure Craft's Bart and Homer ceramic cookie jars released in 1995. The Bart jar is 14 inches high and molded to look like Bart munching on a giant chocolate chip cookie. Bart's head forms the lid of the jar. Even better is the Homer jar. It's 12 inches high and made to look like Homer standing over a barrel, with cookies stuffed into his mouth and the back of his blue pants.

Cheesy: Water bottles

Betras Plastics must have worked its factory overtime in 1990 turning out millions of Simpsons water bottles. Nine years later, they remain a mainstay of garage sales and flea markets.

This drinking container leaks. It has no insulation. It gives water a plastic aftertaste. No wonder so many remain unused. The best thing that can be said about these water bottles is that they typically cost only a buck or two.

Bart Simpson "Radical Dude" water bottle, 1990, Betras Plastics. Perhaps the most widely distributed type of Simpsons merchandise.

Stuff to hang

Cool: Calendars

For the first time in three years, U.S. fans in fall 1998 could find a Simpsons calendar in stores. Even better, there were two of them for 1999 — a wall calendar and a desktop calendar.

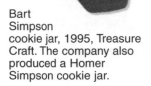

1999 Fun Calendar, 1998, Harper Collins. 24-page calendar with themes for each month. February's theme, for instance, is "12 Types of Love," which includes Homer hugging his TV set.

The Simpsons Fun Calendar, first produced for 1991 by Pantheon, disappeared in the U.S. after 1995, apparently another victim of the decline in popularity of merchandise from the show. Simpsons calendars are real treats — lots of humor and art that undoubtedly have brightened both office walls and children's rooms.

With two more calendars for 2000, there's no need to worry right away about making a date with "The Simpsons."

Cheesy: Automobile window signs

Aging Simpsons fans (anyone older than 15) might remember those yellow "Baby On Board" car-window signs endlessly parodied during the 1980s ("Wife In Trunk," etc.).

In the early 1990s, Bart and the other Simpsons appeared on similarly useless 5-by-5-inch diamond-shaped plastic hangers with suction cups. H&L Entertainment of El Cajon, Calif., which produced these signs, also turned out Simpsons plastic door-knob hangers, wall placards and street signs that had no apparent reason for existence.

Homer Simpson "All-American Dad" automobile window sign, 1990, H&L Entertainment.

Posters

Cool: Tombstone Pizza

In 1994, fans could send away to Tombstone Pizza for a smartly written poster, "Achieving Bartitude." At the center is Bart saying, "The world is my playground, man." Around him are six scenes displaying Bart's advice on living well.

Example: Homer sits at a table, unconscious, with three nearly empty pizza pans in front of him. Bart says,

"On good eating habits: Take it from my old man, never eat more than you weigh." Hilarious — and very Simpsons.

Cheesy: R-rated humor

Cheeky humor is great, but a couple of recent Simpsons posters show off a bit too much. One features an angry-looking Homer pointing to his partially exposed behind and saying, "Kiss my hairy, yellow butt!" Another pictures Bart with his pants to his ankles along with the caption, "Eat my shorts."

The fact that there are also several shirts — and even a wall clock — with similar themes makes one hope Fox has immediate plans for a rear retreat.

"The Simpsons: Songs in the Key of Springfield," 1997, Rhino Records. Check out the song parodies of "Planet of the Apes" and "A Streetcar Named Desire."

Wrapper and card for Simpsons Series II trading cards, 1994, Skybox. Check out the Maggie Simpson card with the scratch-and-sniff diaper.

Kamp Krusty." But even in 1993, anyone younger than 35 would have a hard time getting excited about such guest artists as Linda Ronstadt and George Clinton.

Collectibles

Cool: Skybox trading cards

The scratch-and-sniff, disappearing ink and Arty Art cards are great. But even the "regular" trading cards in Skybox's two Simpsons sets are fun to collect, thanks to cleverly written text and colorful artwork. Much better than the 1990 series from Topps.

Cheesy: Skybox pogs

The pogs phenomenon endured long enough to produce a few Simpsons "collectible" milk caps. Even Groening sounds unimpressed. When asked about his plans for merchandise for his second animated series, "Futurama," Groening specifically promised, "No pogs."

Compact discs

Cool: 'Key of Springfield'

In 1997, Rhino Records released "Songs in the Key of Springfield" a fabulous collection of songs, themes and dialogue from "The Simpsons," including "We Do" (Stonecutter's Song), "Capitol City," the "Itchy & Scratchy Theme," and "Flaming Moe's." The album was a huge hit, inspired a sequel, and proved once again that the best merchandise is tightly linked to content from the show.

Cheesy: 'The Yellow Album'

Maybe if "The Yellow Album" (1998, Geffen) had been released in 1993, when it was recorded, this one wouldn't seem so — well — dated. The album does include a couple of semi-cool tunes, including Apu singing "Twenty-Four Hours a Day" and the entire cast shouting out "Hail to Thee,

"The Yellow Album," 1998, Geffen Records. Recorded for a 1993 release, the album was delayed repeatedly for five years.

Bath items

Cool: Bath 'soakies'

The newest of these British-made bath bottles includes a figure of Marge and Homer in a tub together. Who says this is a dysfunctional family?

Homer and Marge Simpson atop a bottle of bath and shower gel, 1997, Euromark. U.K.

Cheesy: Bart sculpted bath soap

At first, a 3.3-ounce bar of yellow soap shaped like Bart seems kinda cool. Even the packaging is mildly amusing, with such sayings as, "Wash it, dude!" But think about it a second. Do you really want to use a bath soap shaped like a character with spiked hair to clean those delicate places? 'Nuff said.

Outdoor toys

Cool: Bart skateboard

What can you say about a 32-inch board so cool-looking (it includes a skull and crossbones) and wonderfully named — "The Official Bart Simpson Vehicle of Destruction" — that it would be a shame to take it out of its display box, unseal the plastic shrink-wrap, and actually ride it?

Cheesy: Flippy Flyer cloth disc

This ugly 1990 Frisbee wannabe from J.G. Hook is little more than an 8-inch cloth disc showing Bart's head. Even the briskest toss will send it virtually nowhere. This is the quintessential arcade toy — something so awful and useless that the only reason you own one is that you snagged it playing the crane game.

"Official Bart Simpson Vehicle of Destruction" skateboard, 1990, Sport Fun. The 32-inch-long skateboard's top also shows Bart's smiling face.

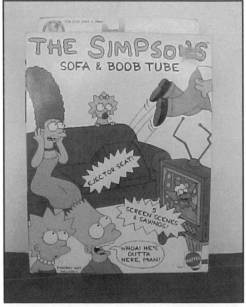

Sofa and Boob Tube accessory, 1990, Mattel. Couch ejector seat and TV. Packaging reads: "It's a sofa on wheels with an ejector seat, plus a TV on wheels with 5 screen scenes and 5 word balloon announcements."

Marge Simpson action figure with word balloons, 1990, Mattel. Packaging reads: "She totes a platter of lovin' from the oven & 5 pieces of advice."

Bartman action figure with word balloons, 1990, Mattel. Packaging reads: "Equipped with cape & super slingshot & 5 tough-talk cards."

Nelson action figure with word balloons, 1990, Mattel. Packaging reads: "He's a bully dude with a trash can & 5 bully-jive cards."

Lisa Simpson action figure with word balloons, 1990, Mattel. Packaging reads: "The sister with a sax & 5 sour notes for Bart."

Maggie Simpson action figure with word balloons, 1990, Mattel. Packaging reads: "She has 5 thoughts to suck on as she cruises on her scooter."

Homer Simpson action figure, 1990, Mattel. Packaging reads: "He has nuke gear for handling hot stuff & 5 words of wisdom."

Bart Simpson action figure with word balloons, 1990, Mattel. Packaging reads: "He's got a custom skateboard & 5 cool quotes."

7 Why collect Simpsons?

There isn't one correct way

Simpsons collecting is a great hobby if you enjoy wearing out shoes wandering through flea markets, if you've got the courage to spend the last of your food money on a rare Lisa doll, and if you don't mind seeing your family life crumble as you dedicate your life to finding all 32 variations of the Simpsons plastic water bottle.

OK, so we exaggerate.

Truth is, Simpsons collecting is also a great hobby if you just want to pick up a few Simpsons trading cards or maybe a Bart figure to plop on your computer monitor at work.

There is certainly no one correct way to pursue Simpsons collecting. While a fan could spend thousands of dollars a year trying to form the ultimate Simpsons collection, others can assemble a credible one for far less.

No matter how much they spend, almost all Simpsons collectors have at least one thing in common. They love "The Simpsons." They are dedicated viewers who make a point of watching each new episode — and often play old ones over and over. While you don't need to be a Simpsons fan to be a Simpsons collector, that would probably be a pretty joyless pursuit. For a typical Simpsons collector, owning a "Really Rude" Bart doll, a Butterfinger watch, or even a Franklin Mint collector plate are alternate ways to enjoy this wonderful show.

Simpsons wrist watch, 1990, Butterfinger candy bars. Part of a mail-in offer. The analog design includes a sweep second hand and a blue plastic strap.

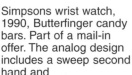

"A Family for the '90s" Simpsons collector plate, 1991, Franklin Mint. From a set of six 8-inch-diameter decorative plates. The porcelain plates are bordered in 24-karat gold.

Vast riches or a money pit?

Even if they don't dwell on it, most collectors have at least a passing interest in the potential investment value of their Simpsons merchandise. If for nothing else, they should know so they can properly insure the collection for its full replacement value.

Simpsons collecting — or any other collecting, for that matter — isn't a certain road to prosperity. The long-term value of Simpsons goods remains unknown. Despite some higher prices recently on the Internet, it's hard to say whether the value for Simpsons toys and other goods will continue to grow.

But we can speculate a bit. And it's a fair guess that the values for carefully preserved Simpsons merchandise will continue to rise. One good reason for believing this is that, until recently, few people have taken Simpsons collecting seriously. For every beautifully preserved Simpsons doll or toy, there were thousands of others used and thrown away. If they do still exist, they tend to be in pretty rotten shape — scuff marks, rips and lack of packaging.

These garage-sale leftovers provide evidence that most buyers didn't hoard Simpsons merchandise. Children ripped

All they can do is read 'em and weep

You have to feel sorry — almost — for people who sank their life savings into comic books a decade ago when they were the latest in hot collectibles. It's sad to think how many people believed they would put their kids through college by buying a comic for $3 and selling it for thousands down the road.

Truth is, many lost a bundle, as did others who saw values plummet for their newly produced "collectible" plates, baseball cards, and "Star Trek" memorabilia.

The good news is that almost no one today sees Simpsons comic books as any kind of serious investment. No hoarding. No price-gouging. In fact, back issues often sell for a buck or two at many comics shops.

Probably this means kids and adults are buying copies to read over breakfast cereal or in the bathtub, and not to slip untouched into plastic covers so they don't get damaged. The irony is that this casual treatment of Simpsons comics — and the enjoyment fans will recall getting from them — could make them much more valuable in 30 years than comics now being pitched as collectibles. But don't bet the kid's college education on it.

the toys out of the packaging and had a ball playing with them. This probably explains why it's hard to find early Simpsons toys in any kind of decent shape. That shortage of "mint condition" toys already is pushing up typical prices.

But what about future demand? "The Simpsons" definitely fits the general profile of past pop-culture phenomena whose licensed goods have become extremely popular over time. Like "Lost in Space" and "The Brady Bunch," "The Simpsons" has strong appeal to kids between the ages of 10 and 17 — a time in their lives they'll want to recapture in their 30s and 40s.

The one difference is that "The Simpsons" also appeals to adult viewers. That's a variable that might make the show's merchandise eventually fall more in line with the lasting popularity of "Star Wars" and "Star Trek" merchandise.

The few, the proud

Right now, though, collecting Simpsons merchandise remains the passion of a relatively few souls. A visit to any toy or collectibles show is likely to hammer this point home. For every table sporting a solitary Bart doll or key ring, there are dozens of other tables piled high with Beanie Babies, or licensed merchandise from "Star Wars," "Star Trek" and NASCAR.

In fact, at any typical toy show, you're more likely to find a bigger selection of items from the 1960s than from "The Simpsons."

It's reasonable to expect this secondary status for Simpsons merchandise to vanish over the next decade.

Or perhaps not.

Maybe Twentieth Century Fox will flood the U.S. market with Simpsons toys in such a way that it depresses prices for the early stuff. Or people will just — aye carumba! — lose interest in "The Simpsons."

In any case, the old axiom holds true here that people should only collect stuff they really like. They can still be happy with their collection, even if they're the only ones who think it's worth anything.

8 Getting the goods

Around the world with Simpsons merchandise

A surge of Simpsons toys and other goods in Europe and Australia in the late 1990s is great news for fans there. But finding Simpsons merchandise in the United States is still about as easy as getting Homer's religious neighbor Ned Flanders to curse.

Despite the show's continued popularity in the U.S., there are almost no Simpsons goods in this country's retail stores — or even at collectibles shops and toy shows.

Flea markets and garage sales remain potential sources for older Simpsons items, such as board games and dolls, but finding anything is a hit-and-miss (mostly miss) proposition. Prices are usually reasonable. However, the condition of these used items is typically poor, making them less than desirable to collectors who prefer items in mint condition.

Other sources for Simpsons items are small-town stores with slow-moving inventories, dollar stores and comic shops, although even these places offer few items.

Toy Shop magazine and other collector publications sometimes carry advertisements for Simpsons items from dealers and other collectors. But prices rarely are bargains, even for newer items.

It's a cyber-Simpsons world

For those seeking Simpsons merchandise, the Internet is now the best source. At least a half-dozen Web sites focus exclusively on selling Simpsons goods.

Other places to find Simpsons merchandise are for-sale notes on Internet newsgroups. The best places to look include alt.tv.simpsons, rec.toys.misc and rec.collecting.

By far, the hottest spot to buy and sell Simpsons merchandise on the Internet is the eBay auction site at www.ebay.com. At eBay, collectors can typically scroll through lists of 600 or more Simpsons items for sale from private collectors and others.

Although competition among sellers on eBay keeps prices for common Simpsons items at a reasonable level, expect to pay some wallet-draining prices for hard-to-find merchandise, such as the Simpsons Score-O-Matic pinball machine. That game sold not long ago for more than $200.

As with any purchase, comparison shopping is a good idea. Because buyers and sellers are often unaware of the typical values for Simpsons items, prices vary widely. Review the prices listed in this book or check for updates at the Collecting Simpsons! Web site (http://members.aol.com/bartfan).

Q&A

The Collecting Simpsons! Web site regularly answers e-mail from readers looking for information on where to find merchandise. Here are some answers posted on the Web site to a few frequently asked questions:

Q: Where can I find older issues of Simpsons comics?

A: The publisher, Bongo Comics, doesn't offer subscriptions or back issues. Your best bet is to check out the back-issue bin at comic-book stores. Assuming that's not an option or you've already tried that, check out the Internet, where you can place a want-to-buy note on one of the comic-book or collector newsgroups. Or use Yahoo! (www.yahoo.com) or one of the Internet

Simpsons Illustrated Issue No. 1, Spring 1991. The officially licensed magazine folded in 1993, but those 11 issues remain sought-after collector items.

search engines to locate an online comic-book store.

Q: **Where can I find Simpsons Illustrated?**

A: The official Simpsons magazine went out of business several years ago. But you can sometimes find back issues for sale on the Internet.

Q: **Where can I find Simpsons bank checks?**

A: Manufacturer Deluxe discontinued its line of Simpsons checks in spring 1998. As of this writing, no other company was offering them.

Q: **How do I write series creator Matt Groening to get his autograph?**

A: The best address seems to be:
The Simpsons
c/o Twentieth Television
Matt Groening's Office
P.O. Box 900
Beverly Hills, CA
90213
The same address will probably work for others with the show.

Q: **Any idea where to find Homer and Marge wedding cake toppers?**

A: No. Apparently, no company has produced them, although an artistic person might be able to dress up regular action figures of Homer and Marge for such a purpose.

Q: **Are there any Simpsons Halloween costumes?**

A: Finding Simpsons costumes in U.S. stores isn't easy, as they haven't been produced in this country for several years. But costume shops and Halloween stores might have some left in their inventories.

Q: **Why don't I see dolls featuring popular Simpsons characters such as Sideshow Bob, Mr. Burns, Waylon Smithers, Ned Flanders, etc.?**

A: Fox has mostly licensed merchandise featuring Bart, Homer and the other family members. The studio apparently feels these characters have the broadest appeal and would sell the most merchandise. However, keep looking, because merchandise with other characters sometimes pops up. One example is Krusty the Clown, where at least two different dolls have been produced.

Q: **Where can I find a Simpsons T-shirt?**

A: The most convenient place is probably your local T-shirt shop. If it doesn't have what you want, you might try Internet merchants, although shipping costs for small orders will add considerably to the cost.

Simpsons Wave 2 Triple Pack box set, 1997, Fox Home Video. This three-cassette set features six Simpsons episodes and three Simpsons shorts from "The Tracey Ullman Show."

Q: **I'm looking for copies of episodes not yet on home video. Where can I get them?**

A: Your best bet is to either catch reruns in syndication or to wait until they are released by Fox Home Video. Some fans swap tapes in Internet newsgroups, although doing so is of questionable legality and sometimes results in getting copies of poor quality.

Q: **Where can I find the best deals on Simpsons animation cels? Are they worth the high prices I've seen?**

A: Simpsons animation cels are a great way to own a piece of something actually used in making the series. But it's wise to do a lot of research before buying. A good place to start is our next chapter on animation cels.

Bartman watches, 1990, Nelsonic. 8-inch-long blue band and 9½-inch-long black band with larger watch face. Both have flip-up covers.

Simpsons wallet, 1996, Copywrite. UK. Originally sold in this sealed bag.

Bart Simpson "Cowabunga dude!" hair clip, 1990, Wow Wee Products. Canada. 2¾ inches wide.

Bart Simpson Heirloom Collection holiday ornament, 1998, Carlton Cards. This 3½-inch hard-plastic figure was the first in a new series of ornaments.

Homer Simpson Heirloom Collection holiday ornament, 1999, Carlton Cards. 4-inch-high hard-plastic figure. Fine in detail, there's even raised glitter on the white border of the Santa Claus suit

Bart and Homer Simpson pencil toppers, 1997, Vivid Imaginations. U.K. 7-inch pencils with a figure of Bart and Homer on top. The design on the pencils shows Bart and Homer in various poses.

9 Animation art

The big picture

Let's begin with a short quiz.

What is an "animation cel"?

A. A component of living tissue that moves around a lot.

B. A room in a prison for people who make cartoons.

C. Hand-painted scenes on plastic cellulose acetate or cellulose nitrate that are photographed in sequence to create the movement of a cartoon.

If you answered "**C**," give yourself a big Frinkian pat on the back. (Insider-reference clue: Professor Frink is the genius scientist on "The Simpsons.")

For many Simpsons fans, animation art is the filet mignon of collectibles. Pricey, yes, but definitely a tasty, high-class item.

Almost any Simpsons production cel — matted and framed, of course — can put sparkle into even the dullest of antiques-laden rooms. The fact that many people believe cels have great investment potential only adds to their luster, especially if it persuades a skepti-

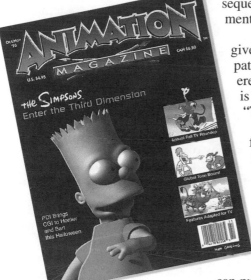

Animation magazine, October 1995. The issue offers the cover story, "The Simpsons Enter the Third Dimension," with a shot of a 3-D Bart from that fall's Halloween episode.

cal spouse it's worth $300 or more to buy one. (There are also limited-edition cels created for collectors, but we'll get to those shortly.)

Not everyone thinks hanging a drawing of Homer Simpson in the living room meets the definition of fine decorating. But it's hard to find any owner of a Simpsons cel who regrets having one on display.

The making of 'The Simpsons'

To understand Simpsons animation art, it helps to know the process for making an episode.

After writers create a script, the voice actors such as Nancy Cartwright ("Bart") and Harry Shearer ("Mr. Burns") record the dialogue.

Next, the show's artists draw "story boards," which look much like black-and-white panels of a comic book. These drawings guide animators in creating "master drawings." About 16,000 sketches are needed for each half-hour episode. These drawings, filmed one after another, create a rough "animatronic" version of the episode.

The sketches are shipped to a studio in Korea, where outlines of each drawing are copied onto clear plastic and filled in with paint. These are called "cels," which in sequence produce the spiffy animation seen on television. In many cases, an

ces:
ito,
also
r a

A story board from an early Simpsons short, as published in a behind-the-scenes story in the spring 1991 premiere issue of Simpsons Illustrated magazine.

artist only has to draw the foreground art of a cel. A single "master background" is used for several cels in the same scene.

The business of animation art

There was a time not so long ago when studios discarded cels after a cartoon was created because they thought the individual art was worthless. These days, animation cels are guarded by studios as valuable property, often promoted to the public as works of art.

Cels from "The Simpsons" are certainly big business, fueled in part by soaring prices at auction for animation art from Disney classics and other popular cartoons. Some dealers further promote the market for cels with glossy brochures that pitch them as lucrative investments. A 1996 catalog by the Entertainment Weekly Studio Store, in describing one Simpsons limited-edition cel it sold for $150, called the piece a "true collectible whose value will only increase."

Serious art or not — and there are many who don't believe modern cartoon qualifies as serious art — cels definitely carry rarefied prices compared with most other pieces of Simpsons merchandise. Prices typically range from about $300 for an unframed production cel to $2,000 for a limited edition.

But even these price tags don't come close to what some collectors paid for the first Simpsons cels sold to the public.

The big Simpsons art auction

Lots of hoopla surrounded Twentieth Century Fox Film Corp.'s first public sale of Simpsons cels. On June 20, 1991, the studio offered 27 of them at auction at Christie's East in New York City. Each cel came with its own hand-painted background and each was signed by series creator Matt Groening.

Auction officials expected these cels to sell for $800 to $1,000 each. But when the final bid was in from the 500 people on hand, the average price was $4,211.

The highest bid — $24,200 — nabbed a cel showing Bart auctioning off sister Maggie. Ironically, it wasn't even a production cel. The piece was produced for the cover of the auction catalog. New York restaurateur Antonio Francesco, an art collector, bought this one and several other Simpsons cels.

But it was Ross Krasnow, 9, of North Bay Village, Fla., who found himself at the center of media attention for his winning bid of $4,950 for a cel from the episode "The Crepes of Wrath." When USA Today asked the boy if he bought the piece with savings from his piggy bank, Ross replied, "No, with my dad's money."

Galleries become source for cels

Later in 1991, Twentith Century Fox began shipping Simpson cels — minus hand-painted backgrounds — to animation galleries.

Today, there are hundreds of Simpsons cels to choose from, although a fan would be wise not to pin hopes on finding a Simpsons production cel featuring a particular scene, a famous guest or even a favorite episode.

Fox releases selected batches of Simpsons cels only about three or four times a year, according to Debbie Weiss, owner of the Wonderful World of Animation gallery in New York City. And each of these releases only amounts to about 200 cels.

"Which as you may imagine is not a lot, considering that they have to satisfy the worldwide demand for Simpsons animation art," Weiss wrote in 1998 in Collectables, a magazine published in the United Kingdom. Weiss also notes that Fox only releases to the public production cels from episodes that are several years old, so don't bother looking for one from the last year or two.

Types of Simpsons art

When it comes to Simpsons cels, not all art is created equal. Cels fall into three main categories.

Choosing the right one means considering price, as well as personal taste.

Original production cels

Many Simpsons collectors favor original cels because they want something actually used to make an episode of the show.

"Wouldn't you rather have a small piece of an episode that you really enjoyed over a limited edition that was produced only to produce profit?" one fan told the Collecting Simpsons! Web site. "For me one of the neat things about production cels is to be able to match up the cel to the exact frame on a tape (of an episode)."

Each production cel is unique — even those from the same scene — because of differences in expressions of the characters, size of images or overall attractiveness of the particular cel. Some cel buyers are surprised to find out that production-cel art isn't that big. A typical cel size is 10-by-12 inches.

Although initially Fox released Simpsons cels with their original master backgrounds, the studio hasn't done so in recent years. They now ship cels with reproduction backgrounds. Because of their rarity, cels with original backgrounds command higher prices. Prices for most production cels range from $400 to $600, with ones featuring Homer and Bart typically the most expensive.

Limited-edition sericels

Also called "serigraph cels," these are silk-screened works carefully created by adding individual colors to the cel, one at a time. This gives the cel a flawless look.

Simpsons sericels are generally produced in quantities of 2,500. Their relatively large production makes them the most affordable of Simpsons cels.

The first Simpsons sericel was "Bart-O-Lounger," which commemorated the 100th episode of the show. That one, which originally sold for about $150, is no longer available from most dealers. A more recent sericel, "Simpsons On-

Line," is about 3 feet long and features 20 characters from the show. Typically priced at about $300, this one also has an edition size of 2,500.

Limited-edition hand-painted cels

Like production cels, these are painted by hand. But they never were used to make an episode of "The Simpsons." The studio creates these cels in relatively small numbers, often in quantities of 500 or less.

Because of work involved in designing and creating them, prices are usually higher than any other type of Simpsons animation art. For instance, a limited edition featuring art from six "Treehouse of

The first limited-edition Simpsons sericel, "Bart-O-Lounger," 1996, Fox. A limited edition of 2,500, the sericel was originally sold in a 20-by-17-inch frame for about $150. It includes a certificate of authenticity.

Horror" specials had an original selling price of $2,500, framed and bearing Matt Groening's autograph. The edition size for this one is 300.

Like other licensed cels, one piece inspired by the "Who Shot Mr. Burns?" two-part episode featured an official seal and a certificate of authenticity. But as a bonus, it also came with a giant yellow folder containing press releases, a T-shirt with graphics from the episodes, and a magnifying glass with "Who Shot Mr. Burns?" printed on the handle.

Art of the deal

As with all collectibles, especially those as pricey as animation art, it's a smart idea to do some homework before buying.

"Always compare when buying cels," one cel owner emphasizes. "A lot of dealers drool at the chance to rip off newbies. Do your research. Learn about the art form. The best consumer is an educated consumer. Do not ever let anyone pressure you!"

Be particularly careful in buying by mail, especially when an individual offers a cel for what seems like an unusually great price. The cel might be damaged, unlicensed or even a homemade reproduction.

Do comparison shopping

The safest bet in buying any cel is to find a reputable gallery — or at least a seller who lives nearby so you can inspect the cel in person.

Luck can also play a role in landing a good deal. Eric, a Simpsons fan, told Collecting Simpsons! he spent hours in informal research before buying his first cel. He did comparison shopping. He checked out information on the Internet and elsewhere.

Then one day he was attending an animation art show. He overheard a woman talking to an art dealer. The woman was trying to sell a Simpsons production cel picturing Bart and Lisa watching television while Maggie crawls toward them.

Eric knew from his research that price tags for similar cels featuring all three of the Simpsons children ranged from $600 to $700. The dealer hesitated. Eric made his move. "He (the dealer) told her to come back later that afternoon. I followed her out and anxiously told her that I might be interested," Eric recalls. "Once I saw the cel, I knew I had to have it. It was by far the best cel I had seen of the kids."

The woman sold the piece to Eric for $300. And now this Simpsons cel — matted, framed and displaying the official Twentieth Century Fox gold seal on the front — hangs prominently in his office. "Everyone who sees it for the first time goes nuts over it," Eric says.

Investment potential of cels

Profit is almost a dirty word to some Simpsons cel collectors. "I have over 30 cels and I have never bought one of them for an investment," Eric says. "Just because a book or an expert tells you your art is worth $1,000, that doesn't mean you'll find a seller. You need to love the artwork you buy. If you do end up selling it, hopefully it will be worth more, but don't count on it!"

Some collectors believe almost all production cels will become more valuable as studios turn to computer-generated cels to replace hand-painted drawings. However, Forbes magazine warned as early as 1993 that prices were becoming "overheated" and were likely to fall as more and more products became available.

"There's lots of this stuff around, and once the demand is satisfied prices could drop sharply," the magazine wrote. So far, though, prices for Simpsons art show little sign of collapsing, in part because Fox has released relatively few cels.

On the other hand, it's hard to find any case where a Simpsons cel is selling for more than its original price. In fact, collectors selling Simpsons cels on the Internet tend to set asking prices less than newer art selling at galleries.

This recent history gives credibility to advice from Forbes and others. As Eric puts it, "Anyone interested in buying cels or any type of art as an investment is wasting their time."

"Garden of Eden" sericel, 1998, Fox. Unframed artwork from this limited edition of 1,200 pieces. It comes with its own certificate of authenticity. Typically, this cel is sold in galleries for about $150, with an extra charge for framing.

Simpsons merchandise price guide

So how much is that Bart Simpson doll really worth? How old is the Homer cookie jar? Did that Bart pajama bag originally come with packaging?

Welcome to the Simpsons Merchandise Price Guide. This section is devoted to detailed information on more than 1,000 Simpsons items. Here you'll find typical prices for goods released in the United States and other countries.

The listings for most items include:
■ An original copyright date. (This typically is the year the item was manufactured.)
■ The name of the manufacturer.
■ A brief description of the item.
■ The type of original packaging.

Unless noted, items listed were originally sold in the United States.

Packaging descriptions

If packaging exists for an item, its listing will include one of the following notations:
"Sealed." Shrink-wrapped or sealed in a plastic wrapper.
"Bagged." Contained in a bag.
"Carded." Attached to a display card.
"Boxed." Packaged in a display box.
"Framed." Held by a frame.
"Rolled." Packaged in rolled form.
"Tagged." Attached to a display tag.

If one of these notations isn't included, it means the item was found without any packaging.

These are typical prices

The first dollar amount listed with each item is an approximate value in "mint" condition without packaging.

The second figure is the value of the item in mint condition with "near-mint"

original packaging, if such packaging exists. For items without packaging or in lesser condition, typical prices are usually much lower.

While it's true that collectors can sometimes pay more or less for Simpsons merchandise than the prices in this guide, the amounts do reflect typical selling prices recently.

Defining mint condition

This book uses the common definition among collectors for "mint" condition. That means the toy or other item has absolutely no flaws. No wrinkles. No dirt marks. No fading. It is perfect, just as it came off the assembly line.

While it's pretty easy to find Simpsons toys in that condition, their packaging rarely meets that standard. Even packaging on toys in stores rarely stays that way.

That's why this book lists values for packaging that's in "near mint" condition — which means it may show very minor wear but is otherwise like new.

Most collectors seek mint items with original packaging, which accounts for the higher values than those items without packaging.

This book isn't a catalog

Be aware that items in the Price Guide are NOT for sale from the author. These items are listed for informational purposes. The listings shouldn't be interpreted as an offer to buy, sell or trade.

If you are looking to buy Simpsons merchandise, be sure to consult other chapters in this book offering suggestions on where to purchase it.

Family on sofa dining placemat, 1990, Trends International Corp. 11-by-17-inch coated paper. Bart is saying, "I have an announcement to make, I'm bored."

Family wall clock, 1990. JPI. 11-inch-diameter oval clock shows the Simpsons making peace signs over each others' heads. Requires one AA battery, not included. Originally sold in sealed cardboard and plastic.

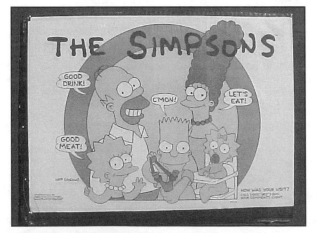

Burger King placemat. This 10-by-14-inch paper placemat arrived on trays with meals served during the restaurant chain's 1990 Simpsons promotion. The Simpsons are variously saying "Good drink!" "Good meat!" "C'mon!" "Let's eat!".

10 Action figures

Mattel

Bart action figure, 1990. Movable joints, word balloons and accessories. "He's got a custom skateboard & 5 cool quotes." Carded. . . . .$5-$25.

Bartman action figure, 1990. Movable joints, word balloons and accessories. "Equipped with cape & super slingshot & 5 tough-talk cards." Carded. . . . . . .$5-$25.

Homer action figure, 1990. Movable joints, word balloons and accessories. "He has nuke gear for handling hot stuff & 5 words of wisdom." Carded. . . . . . .$7-$30.

Lisa action figure, 1990. Movable joints, word balloons and accessories. "The sister with a sax & 5 sour notes for Bart." Carded. . . . .$10-$35.

Maggie action figure, 1990. Movable joints, word balloons and accessories. "She has 5 thoughts to suck on as she cruises on her scooter." Carded. . . . .$5-$25.

Marge action figure, 1990. Movable joints, word balloons and accessories. "She totes a platter of lovin' from the oven & 5 pieces of advice." Carded. . . . .$5-$25.

Nelson action figure, 1990. Movable joints, word balloons and accessories. "He's a bully dude with a trash can & 5 bully-jive cards." Carded. . . . .$5-$25.

Sofa and Boob Tube, 1990. Accessory to the action figures. "It's a sofa on wheels with an ejector seat, plus a TV on wheels with 5 screen scenes and 5 word balloon announcements." Carded. . . . .$35-$50.

Bart Action Wind Up, 1990. 3-inch-high figure on wind-up car. Red and green variations. Carded. . . . .$10-$30.

Lisa Action Wind Up, 1990. 3-inch-high figure on wind-up car. Carded. . . . .$10-$30.

Maggie Action Wind Up, 1990. 3-inch-high figure on wind-up rocking horse. Carded. . . . .$10-$30.

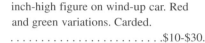

Lisa Simpson Action Wind Up figure, 1990, Mattel. The other side of the figure includes a knob to wind it up.

Dan Dee

Bart Collectible Figure, 1990. 6-inch-high figure. Green cloth body and a plastic head. Carded. . . . .$15-$20.

Homer Collectible Figure, 1990. 7½-inch-high figure. Cloth body and a plastic head. White shirt has "Homer" printed on left breast pocket. Carded. . . . . .$15-$20.

Lisa Collectible Figure, 1990. 6-inch-high figure. Green cloth body and a plastic head. Carded. . . . .$15-$20.

Maggie Collectible Figure, 1990. 5-inch-high figure. Pink cloth body and a plastic head. Carded. . . . . . .$15-$20.

Marge Collectible Figure, 1990. 9-inch-high figure. Cloth body and a plastic head. Marge wears an apron that says, "Kiss the chef." Carded. . . .$15-$20.

Bartman clip-on figure, 1990, Dan Dee. The company produced a similar figure featuring Bart without his superhero costume.

Four of five of Jesco's Simpsons Bendable Action Figures, 1990. The fifth one, not pictured, is a very bulky Homer.

Other

Clip-on, Bart, 1990. Dan Dee. Vinyl. 5-inch-high with arms that grasp. Carded. . . . .$2-$8.

Clip-on, Bartman, 1990. Dan Dee. Vinyl. 5-inch-high with arms that grasp. Carded. . . . . .$3-$10.

Gift collection, family, 1997. Vivid Imaginations. U.K. Six 1-to-3-inch-high figures of Homer, Marge, Bart, Lisa, Maggie and Krusty the Clown. Boxed. . . . .$10-$25.

KFC 4-piece 3D Diorama Sandcastle, 1998. Kentucky Fried Chicken. Pieces shaped like Simpsons family snap together. Bagged. $10-$20.

PVC figure, 4-inch Bart skateboarding, 1990. Bagged. . . . .$2-$5.

PVC figure, 3-inch Bart skateboard, 1990. Bagged. . . . .$2-$5.

PVC figure, 3-inch Bart playing air guitar, 1990. Bagged. . . . .$2-$5.

PVC figure, 2½-inch Bart playing air guitar, 1990. Bagged. .$2-$5.

PVC figure, 4½-inch Homer holding football, 1990. Bagged. . . .$2-$5.

PVC figure, 3½-inch Homer holding football, 1990. Bagged. . . . . .$2-$5.

PVC figure, 3-inch Lisa, arms outstretched, 1990. Bagged. . . . .$2-$5.

PVC figure, 2-inch Maggie with ice cream, 1990. Bagged. . . . .$2-$5

PVC figure, 3½-inch Marge, with cat on leg, 1990, ...$2-$5.

Rev 'N' Go Racer, Bart, 1990. Arco. Bart in small car that springs forward after rolling it in reverse. Carded. . . . .$5-$20.

Rev 'N' Go Racer, Homer, 1990. Arco. Homer in small blue car that springs forward after rolling it in reverse. Carded. . . . .$5-$20.

Subway restaurant, 3-inch Bart wind-up, 1997. On skateboard. Bagged. . . . . $2-$7.

Subway restaurant, 2-inch Bartman, 1997. Spins inside a frame. Bagged. . . . .$2-$7.

Subway restaurant, 3-inch Homer, 1997. Chases after large donut. Bagged. . . . .$2-$7.

Jesco

Bart Bendable Action Figure, 1990. 4½ inches. Carded. . . . .$3-$10.

Homer Bendable Action Figure, 1990. 6 inches. Carded. . . . .$4-$10.

Lisa Bendable Action Figure, 1990. 3½ inches. Carded. . . . .$4-$12.

Marge Bendable Action Figure, 1990. 6 inches. Carded. . . . .$3-$10.

Maggie Bendable Action Figure, 1990. 2½ inches. Carded. . . . .$8-$10.

Set of five Bendable Action Figures, 1990. Same figures together. Boxed. . . . .$15-$35.

Burger King

Bart camping figure, 1990. With overstuffed back pack. Bagged. . . . .$1-$3.

Homer camping figure, 1990. Holding up sock, with skunk next to him. Bagged. . . . .$1-$3.

Lisa camping figure, 1990. Playing saxophone, next to bunny. Bagged. . . . .$1-$3.

Maggie camping figure, 1990. Sitting on turtle. Bagged. . . .$1-$3.

Marge camping figure, 1990. Holding binoculars. Bagged. . . . .$1-$3.

Cardboard background camping scenes, 1990. Five styles. Sealed. . . . .$3-$7 each.

Homer Simpson action figure, 1990, Burger King. Which smells worse, the skunk or Homer's sock?

Lisa Simpson action figure, 1990, Burger King. Part of a set of 5 camping figures.

Marge Simpson PVC action figure with Snowball II. Released in early 1990s.

Bart Simpson action figure, 1990, Burger King. Originally sold in sealed bag.

Subway restaurant, 4-inch Lisa, 1997. Blowing a saxophone-shaped whistle. Bagged. . . . .$2-$7.

Vivid Imaginations, 4½-inch Bart bendable, 1997. U.K. Carded.

. . . .$5-$12.

Vivid Imaginations, 6-inch Homer bendable, 1997. U.K. Carded.

. . . .$5-$12.

Winchell's donut shops, 6½-inch Homer, 1993. Homer holds 2 donuts above his head. Includes sticker set with "sayings of donut ambassador Homer Simpson." Bagged. . . . . . .$3-$10.

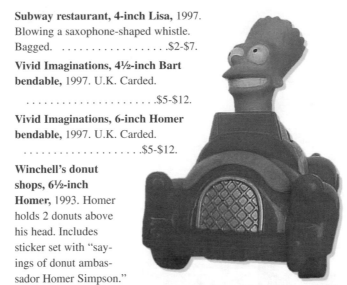

Bart Simpson Rev 'N' Go Racer, 1990, Arco. Originally sold on a display card.

Winchell's donut shops, 3-inch Bart, 1993. Bart lounges on a huge donut. Includes sticker set with "the sayings of Bart Simpson." Bagged. . . . .$3-$8.

Homer Simpson Rev 'N' Go Racer, 1990, Arco. The back has the sign: "I break (sic) for donuts!"

Four Simpsons figures, 1997, Subway restaurants. From left, Bart on a wind-up skateboard, Lisa with a saxophone that's a real whistle, Bartman spinning in a frame, and Homer chasing a donut.

Bartman figure, 1997, Subway restaurants. 2-inch-high. Bartman spins inside a frame.

Lisa Simpson figure, 1997, Subway restaurants. 4-inch-high. Lisa's saxophone is a real whistle.

Homer Simpson figure, 1997, Subway restaurants. 3-inch-high. Homer chases after donut.

Homer Simpson bendable action figure, 1990, Jesco. Approximately 6 inches high.

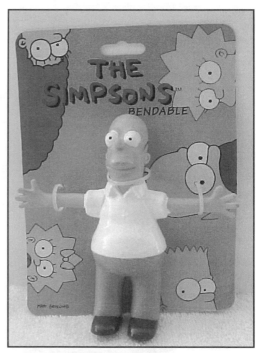

Homer Simpson bendable action figure, 1997, Vivid Imaginations. U.K. Also about 6 inches high and appearing to be indistinguishable from the Jesco bendable. Carded. $5-$12.

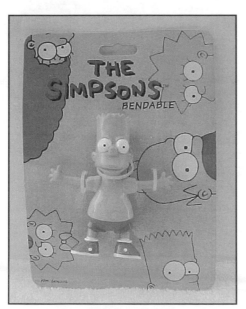

Bart Simpson bendable action figure, 1997, Vivid Imaginations. U.K. Approximately 4½ inches high, and indistinguishable from the 1990 Bart figure from Jesco.

Bart Simpson 11-inch arcade doll, 1990, Acme Premium Supply Co. The doll has a vinyl head and a soft, stuffed body. It's much harder for collectors to find than Acme's 20-inch doll.

Bart Simpson 20-inch arcade doll, 1990, Acme Premium Supply Co. Large vinyl head and furry cloth body. These dolls were typically used as prizes at fairs and arcades.

Lisa Simpson bubble solution, 1990, Mattel. This 4-oz. bottle was sold individually and as an accessory to the "Bubble Blowing" Lisa doll from Mattel.

11 Dolls

Mattel

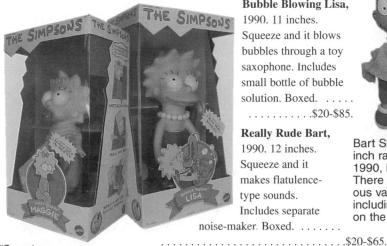

Bubble Blowing Lisa, 1990. 11 inches. Squeeze and it blows bubbles through a toy saxophone. Includes small bottle of bubble solution. Boxed. . . . .$20-$85.

Really Rude Bart, 1990. 12 inches. Squeeze and it makes flatulence-type sounds. Includes separate noise-maker. Boxed. . . . .$20-$65.

"Sweet Suckin'" Maggie and "Bubble Blowing" Lisa Simpson dolls, 1990, Mattel. The set also includes a "Really Rude" Bart doll.

Sweet-Suckin' Maggie, 1990. 10 inches. Squeeze and it sucks non-removable pacifier. Includes play pacifier and play blanket. Boxed. . . . . .$20-$85.

Lisa 15-inch, 1990. All-cloth stuffed rag doll with large plastic eyes. Almost identical to Dan Dee's 15-inch Lisa rag doll, with slightly different packaging in English and Spanish. Boxed. . .$20-$35.

Dan Dee

Bart Pull-String Talking, 1990. 18 inches. Pull cord in back of doll to hear six "smart-aleck" sayings. Variations include plain blue shirt and one with a blue shirt with "Aye carumba!" Boxed. . . . .$18-$80.

Bart 18-inch, 1990. Vinyl head, arms and legs with a soft-stuffed body. Variations include plain blue shirt and one displaying Bart saying, "Don't have a

Bart Simpson 12-inch vinyl doll, 1990, Dan Dee. The company manufactured numerous styles of Bart dolls.

Bart Simpson 18-inch vinyl doll, 1990, Dan Dee. Saving the original cardboard store-display box makes this a complete collectible.

Bart Simpson 10-inch rag doll, 1990, Dan Dee. There are numerous variations, including sayings on the shirt.

cow, man!" Boxed. . . . .$15-$55.

Bart 16-inch, 1990. All-cloth stuffed rag doll with large plastic eyes. Boxed. . .$10-$25.

Bart 12-inch, 1990. Vinyl head, arms and legs with a soft-cloth body. Boxed. . . . .$5-$15.

Bart 12-inch Valentine, 1990. Identical to 12-inch rag doll, except it has red kiss marks on his face. Pink shirt says, "Cooties, man!" Top of display box is heart-shaped. Boxed. .$15-$30.

Bart 10-inch, 1990. All-cloth doll. Variations include a plain blue shirt, one with "Happy Birthday," a blue-and-white shirt with "I (Heart) You," and a blue shirt with "Aye carumba." Carded. . . . .$3-$15.

Bart 10-inch stick-on, 1990. Identical to 10-inch rag doll, except it has tiny suction cups on its arms and feet. Variations include plain blue shirt, one that reads "Aye carumba!" and one that reads "Yo dude." Boxed. . . . .$3-$15.

Bart "Special Expressions," 1990. 10-inch cloth rag doll with green jacket. Carded. . . . .$10-$15.

Homer "Special Expressions," 1990. Cloth rag doll with white bowling shirt. "Homer" is printed on the left breast pocket, and "Barney's Bowlarama" is printed on the back. Carded. . . . .$10-$15.

Lisa 15-inch, 1990. Cloth rag doll with large plastic eyes. Carded. . . . .$10-$30.

Bart Simpson stick-on rag doll, 1990, Dan Dee. The arms and legs feature suction cups so it can hang from inside a car window.

Interview: Yeardley Smith

Yeardley Smith, the voice of Lisa on "The Simpsons," answered a question about Simpsons collectibles in a 1996 interview with this book's author.

Q: Do you own any Lisa dolls and any other merchandise from the show? Do you collect any of that kind of thing?

Yeardley: I collect some. There are some that are very, very good. There's actually not been a lot of Lisa merchandise out there. It really mostly focused on Bart and Homer.

But I did find, about five years ago, a Lisa rag doll that was kind of like a Raggedy Ann, you know. There were six of them, and I bought them all, and that was it. And I never saw them again and they never had them again. And so I still have two of those. I gave away four to several little children over the years who were very, very big fans, and I signed her stomach.

Then my other favorite thing is — I have a little pin ... that is Lisa flying like Superman with a little purple cape wrapped around her neck, and it's very sweet. And they had like five of those left, so I bought all of them, and I've never seen them again. But the stuff that's not done very well doesn't interest me and I don't necessarily collect it just for the sake of it.

Burger King

Bart, 1990. 9-inch with cardboard skateboard. (Tags on all Burger King dolls read in part: "Reg. No. Pa-2530 (HK)") Bagged. . . . .$4-$10.

Homer, 1990. 10-inch with cardboard bowling bag. Bagged. . . . .$4-$12.

Lisa, 1990. 8-inch with cardboard saxophone. Bagged. . . . .$4-$12.

Maggie, 1990. 7-inch with cardboard teddy bear. Bagged. . . . .$4-$10.

Lisa 10-inch, 1990. Cloth rag doll. Carded. . . . .
. . . .$3-$15.

Lisa 10-inch stick-on, 1990. Identical to 10-inch rag doll, except it has tiny suction cups on arms and feet. Boxed. . . . .$5-$20.

Lisa, "Special Expressions," 1990. Identical to 10-inch rag doll, except it features a pink jacket.
. . . .$10-$15.

Lisa and Maggie Simpson stick-on rag dolls, 1990, Dan Dee. These are rag dolls with suction cups on the hands and feet.

Maggie 8-inch, 1990. Cloth rag doll with full-length nightgown and non-removable pacifier. Carded. . . . .$4-$20.

Maggie "Special Expressions," 1990. Identical to 8-inch rag doll except it wears a bib that reads, "Here comes trouble!" Carded. . . . .$10-$15.

Maggie 14-inch, 1990. Cloth doll with with full-length nightgown and non-removable pacifier. Large plastic eyes. Boxed. . . .$20-$35.

Marge, "Special Expressions," 1990. Cloth rag doll with green dress. Carded. . . . .$10-$15.

Marge, 1990. 12-inch with a cardboard purse. Bagged. . . . .$2-$8.

Presents

Bart 6-inch (with slingshot), 1990. Vinyl with gift tag. Faces sideways and holds a slingshot in left hand. Dressed in blue cloth shirt and shorts. Bagged. . . . .$10-$20.

Bart 6-inch (without slingshot), 1990. Vinyl with gift tag. Faces forward with no slingshot. Dressed in blue cloth shirt and shorts. Bagged.
. . . .$10-$20.

Bart 9-inch (with slingshot), 1990. Vinyl with gift tag. Bagged. . . . .$15-$25.

Bart 9-inch (without slingshot), 1990. Vinyl with gift tag. Bagged. . . . .$15-$25.

Homer 7½-inch, 1990. Vinyl with gift tag. White cloth shirt and blue pants. Bagged. . . . .$10-$20.

Lisa 4-inch, 1990. Vinyl with gift tag. Red cloth dress. Bagged. . . . .$10-$20.

Lisa 7-inch, 1990. Vinyl with gift tag. Red cloth dress. Bagged. . . . .$10-$20.

Maggie 4-inch, 1990. Vinyl with gift tag. Blue nightgown and red rattle. Bagged.
. . . .$10-$20.

Marge 9-inch, 1990. Vinyl; with gift tag. Green cloth dress. Bagged. . . . . . .$10-$20.

Vivid Imaginations

Bart "Itchy & Scratchy," 10-inch, 1997. U.K. Soft body with vinyl head. Red T-shirt with image of Itchy and Scratchy. Carded. . . .$10-$20.

Bart "Itchy & Scratchy," 16-inch, 1997. U.K. Soft body with vinyl head. Red T-shirt with image of Itchy and Scratchy. Tagged. . . . . .$20-$30.

Bart, talking, 14-inch, 1997. Soft body with vinyl head. Red T-shirt with image of Itchy and Scratchy. Squeeze its stomach and it says one

Bart Simpson 10-inch "Itchy & Scratchy" doll, 1997, Vivid Imaginations. U.K.

Bart Simpson talking doll, 1997, Vivid Imaginations. U.K. Doll utters three phrases when you squeeze its stomach.

of three phrases: "Eat my shorts!" "Aye, carumba!" or "Gimme a break!" Battery-operated. Boxed. . . . .$35-$50.

Homer Hawaiian, 11-inch, 1997. Soft body with vinyl head. Hawaiian shirt and shorts. Carded. . . . .$15-$20.

Homer Hawaiian, 17-inch, 1997. Soft body with vinyl head. Hawaiian shirt and shorts. Tagged. . . . .$20-$30.

Homer talking, 18-inch, 1997. Soft body with vinyl head. Hawaiian shirt. Squeeze its stomach and it says one of three phrases: "Why you little —," "D'oh!" or "Do I smell cupcakes?" Battery-operated. Boxed. . . . .$35-$50.

Homer Simpson talking doll, 1997, Vivid Imaginations. U.K. Doll utters three phases when you squeeze its stomach.

Other

Bart arcade, 20-inch, 1990. Acme. Vinyl head and furry cloth body. Tagged. . . . .$15-$40.

Bart arcade 11-inch, 1990. Acme. Vinyl head and cloth body. Tagged. . . . .$10-$30.

Homer arcade, 24-inch, 1990. Acme. Vinyl head and furry cloth body. Tagged. . . . .$40-$50.

Homer arcade, 11-inch, 1990. Acme. Vinyl head and cloth body. Tagged. . . . .$15-$20.

Krusty the Clown, 12-inch, 1993. Play-By-Play Toys & Novelties. Bagged. . . . .$10-$30.

Lisa arcade, 10-inch, 1990. Acme. Vinyl head and furry cloth body. Tagged. . . . .$10-25.

Bart bean bag, 7-inch, 1993. Jemini. Vinyl head and cloth body. Boxed. . . . .$15-$25.

Lisa bean bag, 6-inch, 1993. Jemini. Vinyl head and cloth body. Boxed. . . . .$15-$25.

Marge bean bag, 10-inch, 1993. Jemini. Vinyl head and cloth body. Boxed. . . . .$15-$25.

Lisa Simpson arcade doll, 1990, Acme. 10-inch doll that's very close in design to Burger King's Lisa doll.

Lisa Simpson 10-inch rag doll, 1990,
Dan Dee. Cloth body with red felt dress.

Homer Simpson 11-inch arcade doll, 1990,
Acme. Similar in size to Burger King Homer
doll, except the features are somewhat thin-
ner. Cloth body with plastic head.

Homer Simpson Hawaiian-style 11-inch
doll, 1997, Vivid Imaginations. U.K. 11-
inch-high soft body with vinyl head and
Hawaiian-pattern shirt and shorts.

Homer Simpson 17-inch doll with Hawaiian-style clothes, 1997, Vivid Imaginations. U.K. Soft body with vinyl head, the doll is dressed in a Hawaiian-pattern shirt.

Bart Simpson 16-inch doll with "Itchy & Scratchy" T-shirt, 1997, Vivid Imaginations. U.K. Soft body with vinyl head.

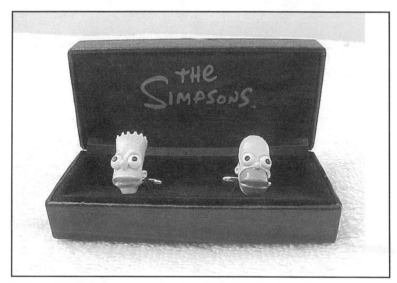

Bart and Homer Simpson cuff links, 1998. U.K. Each is about three-quarters of an inch high. Comes in a 3½-by-1½-inch display box.

Bart doll autopsy

D an Dee's Talking Bart Simpson doll is almost a cultural icon, perhaps the most famous example of Simpsons merchandise. Even Matt Groening's second animated series, "Futurama," had fun in 1999 with this Bart doll by showing a pile of them on a huge ball of garbage from the 21st century.

Truth is, a lot of the Bart dolls do end up in the garbage — often after the pull-string voice box on them begins running too fast. But when one of our talking Barts began sounding a bit like Alvin and the Chipmunks, we decided to do some exploratory surgery to find out a little bit about how it works.

Step One.

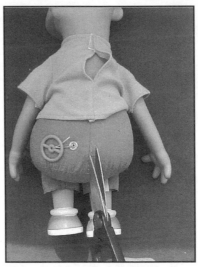

Our scissors cut a 4-inch incision along the seam on the back of the doll, not far from where the plastic ring on the pull string emerges. We chose this spot because it's closest to the voice box and because cutting along the seam would make it easier, if we wanted, to sew up the doll later.

Step Two.

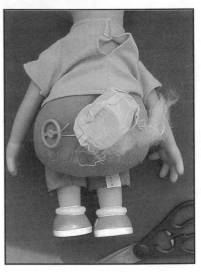

Pushing cotton-like stuffing out of the way, we pull out the voice box that sits inside a white cloth pouch. Because the pull-string is still attached, the box doesn't immediately come loose from the doll. When we pull the string now, the voice sounds a little louder than it did inside the doll.

Step Three.

We cut open the pouch. Inside is the orangish-tan voice box that's about 2½ by 1¾ by 1½ inches. Notice the two screws at one end.

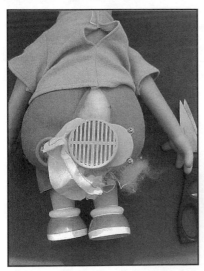

Step Four.

We remove the voice box by snipping the pull string. Had we wanted, we also could have untied the cord from the pull ring.

Step Five.

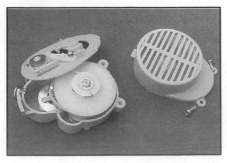

We use a screwdriver to open the box. We don't recommend this step unless the owner doesn't care whether the doll ever talks again. The pieces quickly fall apart when the box is opened, making it almost impossible for an amateur to reassemble it into working shape. The components of the box include a spring, a tiny plastic record with Bart's voice on it, and a needle. When spun along the disc, the needle plays at random six "smart-aleck sayings."

12 Games

Board

Simpsons "Don't Have a Cow" dice game, 1990, Milton Bradley. Board game for two to four players.

3-D Chess Set, 1991. Wood Expressions. Plastic pieces in shapes of Bart (pawn), Marge (queen), Lisa (bishop), Homer (king), Maggie (horse) and Grampa (knight). Boxed. . . . .$25-$45.

3-D Checkers Set, 1994. Wood Expressions. Plastic pieces in shapes of Bart and Lisa. Boxed. . . . .$20-$40

"Don't Have a Cow Dice Game," 1990. Milton Bradley. Contents: eight dice, label sheet, four betting boards, dice cup, playing surface and chips. Object is to win most chips. Boxed. . . . .$10-$20.

"Mystery of Life," 1990. Cardinal. Contents: One game board, dice, four character playing pieces, 40 Simpson check chips, 12 agenda cards, 12 doughnuts, 50 mystery cards, 28 space-related cards, and Simpson bucks. Object is to be the player who gets all five of items on agenda card checked off and back home first. Or player can get home first with 12 doughnuts. Boxed. . . .$10-$20.

"Mystery of Life" deluxe, 1990. Cardinal. Same as regular "Mystery" game, except playing pieces are PVC figures instead of cardboard. Boxed. . . . .$15-$25.

"Bart's House of Weirdness" PC software, 1991, Konami; "Krusty's Super Fun House" PC software, 1993, Acclaim, and "Simpsons Cartoon Studio" CD-ROM software, 1996, Fox Interactive.

PC and Mac software

"Bart's House of Weirdness," 1991. Konami. "Enter the six weird worlds attached to Bart's room and search for the three cool objects." DOS-compatible. Boxed. . . . .$15-$30.

"Krusty's Super Fun House," 1993. Acclaim. "Making Krusty's Fun House vermin-free is not a pretty task." DOS-compatible. Boxed. . .$15-$30.

"The Simpsons Cartoon Studio" CD-ROM, 1996. Fox Interactive. Create brief but slick Simpsons cartoons. Windows- and Macintosh-compatible. Boxed. . . . .$15-$20.

"The Simpsons Arcade Game," 1991. Konami. Based on the full-size arcade game. Bart, Homer, Marge and Lisa fight bad guys to rescue Maggie. 3.5- and 5.25-inch disk versions. DOS-compatible. Boxed. . . .$20-$35.

"Simpsons Screen Saver" CD-ROM, 1994. Berkeley Systems. Animation, music, sound effects, Simpsons voices, 80 icons, 15 classic images. Windows- and Macintosh-compatible. Boxed. . . . .$15-$35.

"Virtual Springfield" CD-ROM, 1997. Fox Interactive. Users click through an interactive Springfield. Windows- and Macintosh-compatible. Boxed. . . . .$20-$30.

"The Simpsons Arcade Game" PC software, 1991, Konami. A DOS-based game based on the full-size video arcade version.

"Simpsons Screen Saver" CD-ROM software, 1994, Berkeley Systems. Spruce up your computer with Simpsons cartoons and real Simpsons

Software reviews

Creating your own Simpsons episodes is no longer a matter of fantasy — or waiting until you've gotten your degree from Harvard so you can join the show's writing staff. No, now you can make slick-looking animation on your personal computer (Macintosh or Windows) using **"The Simpsons Cartoon Studio"** ($34.95, Fox Interactive, 1996.)

With a few clicks of the mouse, you can add, rearrange and remove elements, including music and sound effects. The software also includes more than 10,000 cels of hand-drawn character animation. When you're finished, you can save your Simpsons cartoon short and send it to friends, even if they don't have the "The Simpsons Cartoon Studio" installed. It does take a little while to master this software, but anyone 6 and older should find hours of fun here.

"Virtual Springfield" ($29.95, Fox Interactive, 1997) is truly a gem. Years in the making, this software for Windows and Power Mac computers takes Simpsons fans into a virtual-reality tour of Springfield — from Moe's Tavern to Krustylu Studios.

One particular hoot is the Simpsons home, where you can read Homer's mail or thumb through the family's photo album. This is an engaging 3D animated universe that will consume hours of your time exploring more than 50 interactive locations, many with animated sequences featuring Simpsons characters and original cast voices.

A bit of animated violence and a couple of suggestive moments prompted Fox to give this software an advisory rating of 13-plus. But any parents who let their kids watch "The Simpsons" should have no objections to the content here.

Nintendo

"Bart vs. The Space Mutants," 1990. Acclaim. "A bunch of totally gross monsters are taking over the bodies of the people who live here ..." Boxed. . . . .$15-$30.

"Bart vs. The World," 1991. Acclaim. "Bart's primary goal is to collect the numerous cheap Krusty items that are scattered throughout the countries he visits." Boxed. . . . .$15-$30.

"Bartman Meets Radioactive Man," 1992. Acclaim. Boxed. . . . .$15-$30.

"Krusty's Fun House," 1992. Acclaim. Boxed. . . . .$10-$30.

Game Boy

"Bart Simpson's Escape from Camp Deadly." Nintendo. Boxed. . . . .$15-$30.

"Itchy And Scratchy In Miniature Golf Madness." Nintendo. Boxed. . . . .$15-$30.

"Krusty's Fun House." Nintendo. Boxed. . . . .$15-$30.

"The Simpsons: Bart and the Beanstalk." Nintendo. Boxed. . . . .$15-$30.

"The Simpsons: Bart vs. The Juggernauts." Nintendo. Boxed. . . . .$15-$30.

Super Nintendo

"Krusty's Super Fun House," 1992. Acclaim. Boxed. . . . .$15-$30.

"Virtual Bart," 1994. Acclaim. "Enter the Jurassic era as Dino Bart, and stomp through stone age mayhem." Boxed. . . . .$15-$30.

"Virtual Bart" Super Nintendo game, 1994. Acclaim. One of several Simpsons video games produced for the Super Nintendo system.

"Krusty's Super Fun House" Sega Genesis game, 1992, Flying Edge. One of several Simpsons video games produced for the Sega Genesis system.

Sega Genesis

"Bart's Nightmare," 1993. Flying Edge. Boxed. . . . .$15-$30.

"Bart vs. The Space Mutants," 1992. Flying Edge. Boxed. . . . .$15-$30.

"Krusty's Super Fun House," 1992. Flying Edge. Boxed. . . . . . .$15-$30.

"Virtual Bart," 1993. Acclaim. Boxed. . . . .$15-$30.

Hand-held electronic

"Bart's Cupcake Crisis," 1990. Acclaim. Catch cupcakes Maggie tosses. Carded. . . . .$15-$30.

"Bartman, Avenger of Evil," 1991. Acclaim. Take on Nelson to rescue Maggie. Carded. . . . .$15-$30.

"The Simpsons," 1990. Tiger Electronics. Bart races over obstacles. Carded. $20-$35.

"Talking Bart Vs. Homersaurus," 1994. Tiger Electronics. Voices of Bart and Lisa. Adventure with radioactive dinosaurs. Carded. . . . .$15-$30.

Wrist LCD game, 1990. Tiger Electronics. 1-inch-wide display on wrist band. Shoot paint can out of Homer's hands. Carded. . . . .$12-$25.

"The Simpsons" hand-held electronic game, 1990, Tiger Electronics. Bart tries to evade Nelson, the bully.

"Talking Bart Vs. Homersaurus" hand-held electronic game, 1994, Tiger Electronics. Featuring the real voices of Bart and Lisa.

Electronic toys

Remote Control Quadcycle Bart Simpson, Mattel. Produced in the early 1990s, this vehicle requires two AA batteries (not included).

Pinball, 20 inch battery-operated, 1990. Sharon Industries. Bells ring and lights flash when scoring. Boxed. . . . .$75-$150.

Remote Control Skateboard Bart, 1990. Mattel. 6-inch Bart on skateboard that moves forward, reverses and turns. Battery-operated remote control. Boxed.$25-$50.

Remote Control Quadcycle Bart. Mattel. 3-inch Bart on four-wheeled buggy with remote control. . . . .$30-$60.

Maggie and Bart Simpson mosaic jigsaw puzzles, 1992. Czech Republic. Pictured here are the games' 12-by-6½-inch display boxes.

Mosaic, Maggie, 1992. Czech Republic. Boxed. . . . .$10-$20.

Sliding pieces, Bart, 1990. Ja-Ru. Four 2½-inch square puzzles with pieces that slide to form images. Carded. . . . .$3-$10.

Puzzles

250-piece angry Homer Simpson jigsaw puzzle, 1990, Milton Bradley. An odd design showing the characters in the rough style of the early Simpsons shorts.

Jigsaw, angry Homer. 1990. Milton Bradley. Homer points at an out-of-kilter photograph. 250 pieces. Boxed. . . . .$5-$15.

Jigsaw, Bart on bucking bronco, 1990. Milton Bradley. 250 pieces. . . . .$5-$15.

Jigsaw, Bart water skiing, 1990. Milton Bradley. 250 pieces. Boxed. . . . .$5-$15.

Jigsaw, family at beach, 1990. Milton Bradley. 100 pieces. Boxed. . . . .$3-$12.

Jigsaw, glow in the dark, family, 1997. Zone Products. Australia. 60 pieces. 13-by-12½-inch puzzle showing family members on sofa watching TV. Boxed. . . . .$5-$12.

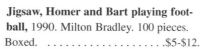

250-piece water-skiing Bart Simpson jigsaw puzzle, 1990, Milton Bradley. He's saying, "Whoa mama!"

Jigsaw, Homer and Bart playing football, 1990. Milton Bradley. 100 pieces. Boxed. . . . .$5-$12.

Jigsaw, family gets picture taken, 1990. Milton Bradley. 100 pieces. . . . . .$5-$12.

Jigsaw, Bart on skateboard with chef Homer, 1990. Milton Bradley. 100 pieces. . . . .$5-$12.

Mosaic, Bart, 1992. Czech Republic. Tiny pieces that can be assembled into a mosaic of Bart. Boxed. . . . .$10-$20.

Two 100-piece Simpsons jigsaw puzzles, 1990, Milton Bradley. Scenes show family posing and Homer tossing a football to Bart.

Pogs (milk caps)

Hypno-Slammers, 1994. Skybox Spin for psychedelic illusion. 10 variations: 1. Psych-O-Delic, 2. Spiralina, 3. Twirly-Gig, 4. Tunnel of Pain, 5. The Mind Bender, 6. Mr. Wobbly, 7. Hypno-Mania, 8. Throbbing Migraine, 9. Swirl-O-Rama, and 10. Whirling Dervish. . . . . .$2 each.

Pogs card set, 1993. DMC. Set of 20 on punch-out card. Instructions on back for playing milk cap game. Carded. . . . .$5-$20.

SkyCaps pogs individual, 1994. Skybox. 50 available featuring Simpsons characters from Skybox trading cards Series I and II. . . .50 cents each.

SkyCaps pogs pack, 1994. Skybox. Foil pack has five pogs, one Hypno-Slammer. Each pack has a SkyCap checklist. Sealed. . . . .$1-$3.

SkyCaps starter kit, 1994. Skybox. Six pogs and one Hypno-Slammer per pack. One cap sealed into lid of case. Sealed. . . . .$1-$3.

SkyCaps Pog Box Set, 1994. Skybox. 24 pogs packs. Sealed. . . . .$20-$30.

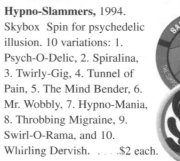

Simpsons pogs and Hypno-Slammers, 1994, Skybox. The designs on the pogs are similar to artwork on Skybox's trading cards of the same year.

Simpsons Action Playset Model Maker, 1990, Rose Art. The display box reads: "Create your own Simpsons family & Bart, too. Three rich colors. Cleaner, neater, smoother ... not a clay. Non toxic."

Simpsons Bio-Genetic Reconstruction Kits, 1997, Caryco Magnets. Two 45-magnet sets, one featuring Bart, Marge and Maggie, and the other with Homer, Lisa and Santa's Little Helper (the family dog).

Crayon-By-Number Set, 1990, Rose Art. Includes six 9-by-12-inch pictures and eight numbered crayons.

Other

Action Playset Model Maker, 1990. Rose Art. Two molds (one Simpsons family mold, one Bart mold) one 9-1/4-inch Action Playmat, three cans of fun dough, modeling tool, plastic modeling knife, and rolling pin. Boxed. . . . .$7-$20.

Velcro darts, 1989. Ben Cooper. 30-by-18-inch wall-mount game using Velcro-wrapped balls as darts. Boxed. . . . .$25-$35.

Beauty bag toy set, Marge, 1990. Mattel. Includes 6-inch-long vinyl pouch with zipper and strap, small mirror, "Marge's perfume" bottle, hair brush, comb, a bottle labeled "Marge's hair stuff," and tiny hair rollers and clips. Boxed. $20-$40.

Bio-Genetic Reconstruction Kit, Marge, Bart and Maggie, 1997. Caryco Magnets. 45 magnets with Simpsons body parts to create mutant variations. Sealed. . . . .$8-$15.

Bio-Genetic Reconstruction Kit, Homer, Lisa and Santa's Little Helper, 1997. Caryco Magnets. 45 magnets with Simpsons body parts to create mutant variations. Sealed. . . . .$8-$15.

Bopper bag, Bart, 1990. Helm Toy. 12-inch-high inflatable bag that returns to standing position after punched. Boxed. . . . .$5-$20.

Frisbee-like Simpsons flying disc, 1991, Butterfinger BB's candy.

Bopper bag, Homer, 1990. Helm Toy. 12-inch-high inflatable bag that returns to standing position after punched. Boxed. . . . . $5-$20.

Bubbles solution, Lisa's, 1990. Mattel. 4 oz. bottle. Sealed. . . . .$5-$12.

Chocolate quiz game, 1997. St. Michael. U.K. Trivia game played using wrappers for 14 milk chocolates. Boxed. . . . .$15-$20.

Colorforms, Deluxe Play Set, 1990. Colorforms. Plastic pieces stick to board to create Simpsons scenes. Boxed. . . . .$10-$20.

Simpsons Hot Wheels Family Camper and Hot Wheels Nuclear Waste Van, 1990, Mattel. Different scenes inside-based on the color of the hubs.

Colorforms, Play Set, 1990. Colorforms. Plastic pieces stick to board to create Simpsons scenes. Smaller board than deluxe set. . . . .$8-$18.

Crayon-By-Number, 1990. Rose Art. Six 9-by-12-inch pictures and eight numbered crayons. Boxed. . . . . . .$5-$20.

Design N' Wear Magic Paint T-shirt design kit, 1990. Rose Art. Five bottles of paint, two iron-on transfers to paint, two artist brushes. Boxed. . . . . .$5-$20.

Flip Face, Bart, 1990. Ja-Ru. Flip buttons on tiny box to make combination of faces of Homer, Bart and Lisa. Carded. . . . .$2-$10.

Flippy Flyer, Bart "Watch it, dude!" 1990. J.G. Hook. 8-inch cloth disc you toss like a Frisbee. . . . . .$7.

Simpsons velcro darts, 1989, Ben Cooper. On top it reads: "The nuclear family game." The Simpsons are pictured next to a nuclear symbol.

Fuzzy Face Homer Simpson game, 1990, Ja-Ru. A magnet with iron filings make Homer look even funnier than usual.

Flying disc, Bart "Radical Dude," 1990. Bettis Plastics. 9-inch Frisbee-like disc. . . . . . .$10.

Flying disc, Bart and Butterfinger BB's, 1991. Butterfinger. Bart pictured saying, "I feel dizzy, man!" . . . .$10.

Fuzzy Face, Homer, 1990. Ja-Ru. Magnetic pencil makes a "fuzzy face" by moving iron filings over Homer's face. Carded. . . . .$2-$10.

Hot Wheels Family Camper, 1990. Mattel. Hold vehicle to your eye to see scene inside. Three scenes, based on whether the hubs are chrome, yellow or blue. Carded. . . . .$3-$10.

Hot Wheels Homer's Nuclear Waste Van, 1990. Hold vehicle to your eye to see scene inside. Three scenes, based on whether the hubs are chrome, yellow or blue. Carded. . . . . . .$3-$10.

Inflatable Wacky Ball, 1990. Mattel. Canada. Bagged. . . . .$3-$10.

Marbles, Collectible Action, 1990. Spectra Star. Six-marble set. Carded. . . . .$3-$10.

Model jet, 1/200th scale of Western Pacific Simpsons logo jet, 1997. Long Prosper. Plastic pieces snap together. Boxed. . . . .$15-$25.

Model jet, 1/500th scale of Western Pacific Simpsons logo jet, 1997. Herpa Wings. Diecast metal replica. 2¾ inches long and 2½ inches wide. Boxed. . . . .$10-$15.

Model jet, 1/600th scale of Western Pacific Simpsons logo jet, 1998. Schabak. Diecast metal replica. 2-¼ inches long and 2 inches wide. Boxed. . . . .$4-$8.

Paddle ball, Bart, 1990. Ja-Ru. Wood paddle with rubber string attached to small red rubber ball. Woolworth logo on some packaging. Sealed. . . . .$5-$10.

Paint By Number Set, 1990. Rose Art. Two 8-by-10-inch pre-printed panels, eight fast-drying acrylic colors, one artist brush, instructions. Boxed. . . . . .$10-$20.

Pinball game on card, 1990. Ja-Ru. 10-by-5-inch plastic game. Carded. . . . .$3-$10.

Playing cards, "Os Simpson," 1991. Fournier. Spain. 33-card deck featuring Simpsons characters. Sealed. . . . .$10-$20.

Pop Gun Target Set, Homer, 1990. Ja-Ru. Plastic squeeze gun, two balls and two Homer targets. Carded. . . . .$2-$10.

Shrinky Dinks Collectible Figures Kit, 1990. Milton Bradley. Color, cut and bake to make 10 figures in four minutes. Boxed. . . . .$5-$15.

Skateboard, "Official Bart Simpson Vehicle of Destruction," 1990. Sport Fun. 32 inches long. Sealed and boxed. . . . .$45-$75.

Simpsons Paint By Number Set, 1990, Rose Art. More proof that "The Simpsons" encourages youthful numbers-crunching.

Simpsons Shrinky Dinks Collectible Figures Kit, 1990, Milton Bradley. The box reads: "Just color, cut & bake to make. In 4 magical minutes, they bake and shrink. ... Place in stands to create 10 figures."

Bart Simpson water squirter, 1990, Mattel. The company also issued similar Homer and Maggie squirters.

Bart Simpson paddle ball, 1990, Ja-Ru. The game was originally sold in a plastic storage pouch.

Stencil Set, Lisa, 1990. Ja-Ru. 5-by-8-inch blue stencil with outlines of Simpsons characters. Includes four crayons and one pencil. Sealed. . . . .$2-$10.

Target Game, Bart, 1990. Ja-Ru. Plastic squeeze gun to shoot four balls at two targets of Homer. Carded. . . . .$3-$10.

Time & Money Kit, Marge, 1990. Ja-Ru. Pretend watch, ring, wallet, credit card and play money. Carded. . . . .$5-$10.

Toss Game & Bop Bag, Bart, 1990. Helm Toy. 48-inch-high inflatable punching bag. One side shows Bart holding up a baseball mitt that opens up to catch four plastic balls. Boxed. . . . .$25-$75.

Trace N' Color Drawing Set, 1990. ToyMax. Trace Simpsons images over a battery-operated light-up box. Includes 6 design sheets, 6 colored pencils, 12 sheets of drawing paper. Boxed. . . . .$20-$35.

Water squirter, Bart, 1990. Mattel. Squeeze 6-1/2-inch plastic figure to squirt water. Carded. . . . .$5-$15.

Water squirter, Homer, 1990. Mattel. Squeeze 7-inch plastic figure to squirt water. Carded. . . . .$5-$15.

Water squirter, Maggie, 1990. Mattel. Squeeze 5-1/2-inch plastic figure to squirt water. Carded. . . . .$5-$15.

Yo-yo, Bart, 1990. Spectra Star. Design shows Bart on skateboard. Carded. . . . .$5-$10.

Bart Simpson yo-yo, 1990, Spectra Star. Packaging reads: "Walk the dog, man!"

Simpsons "Virtual Springfield" CD-ROM software, 1997, Fox Interactive. For Windows 95 and Macintosh, it offers a tour of the Simpsons' home town.

Bart Simpson sliding puzzles, 1990, Ja-Ru. Set of four 2½-inch square puzzles.

Bart Simpson Flip Face game, 1990, Ja-Ru. Push a button on this 4-by-2-inch device to make humorous combinations of the faces of Homer, Bart and Lisa.

"The Simpsons Cartoon Studio" CD-ROM software, 1996, Fox Interactive.
For Windows and Macintosh, it creates brief Simpsons cartoons.

Homer Simpson Pop Gun Target Set,
Homer, 1990, Ja-Ru. Plastic squeeze
gun, two balls and two targets.

Simpsons Trace N' Color Drawing Set,
1990, ToyMax. Trace Simpsons
images over a back-lit table, then
color them.

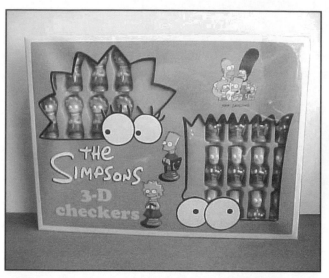

Simpsons 3-D Checkers Set, 1994, Wood Expressions.
Pieces are in the shapes of Bart and Lisa.

Lisa Simpson Double Stamp set, 1989,
Ja-Ru. Six small rubber-style stampers,
two stamp pads and a small booklet
called "My book of stamps."

Diecast metal replicas of Western Pacific Airlines' Simpsons
logo jet. Left, 1/500 scale model, 1997, Herpa Wings. About 2¾
inches long and 2¼ inches wide. Right, 1/600 scale model, 1998,
Schabak. About 2¼ inches long and 2 inches wide. $4-$8.
(Shortly before Western Pacific went out of business in 1998,
the airlines painted over the real-life Simpsons jet.)

Simpsons Deluxe Play Set, 1990, Colorforms. Create scenes with plastic pieces that stick over and over again.

Homer Simpson water squirter, 1990, Mattel. 7-inch hollow plastic. Fill with water and squeeze.

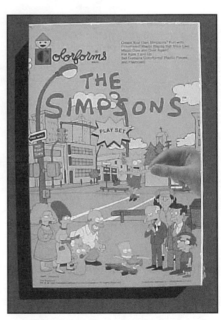

Simpsons Play Set, 1990, Colorforms. Smaller set than deluxe version. Playing board is a street scene.

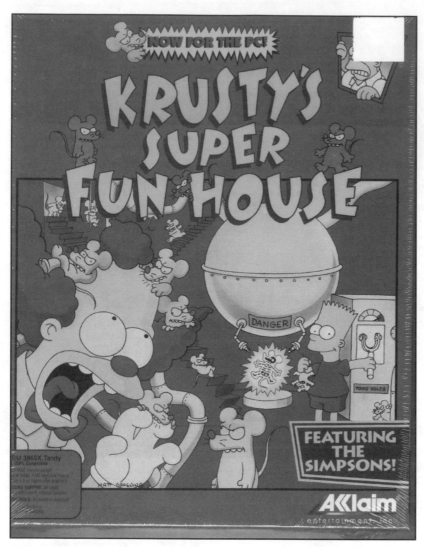

"Krusty's Super Fun House" software, 1993, Acclaim. DOS-compatible game to make Krusty's Fun House vermin-free.

"Bart Vs. The Space Mutants" hand-held video game, 1991, Acclaim. Bart tries to evade mutant creatures.

Maggie Simpson water squirter, 1990, Mattel. 5½-inch hollow plastic. Fill with water and squeeze.

13 Pin, stick and hang

Stickers

Bumper sticker, Bart, "Cowabunga, man!" 1990. NJ Croce Co. . . .$4.

Bumper sticker, Bart, "Don't have a cow, man!" 1990. NJ Croce Co. . . . .$4.

Bumper sticker, Bart, "Outta my way, man!" 1990. NJ Croce Co. . . . .$4.

Bumper sticker, Bart, "Radical dude!" 1990. NJ Croce Co. . . . .$4.

Bumper sticker, Bartman, "Avenger of Evil," 1990. NJ Croce Co. . . . .$4.

Simpsons oval-shaped stickers, 1990. Each is about 6 inches long.

Bartman bumper sticker, 1990, NJ Croce Co. One of several styles of Simpsons bumper stickers, each about 9 by 3 inches.

Bumper sticker, family, "The Simpsons Workout," 1990. NJ Croce Co. . . . .$4.

Bumper sticker, Lisa, "Overachiever," 1990. NJ Croce Co. . . . .$4.

Bumper sticker, Maggie, "World's Best Baby," 1990. NJ Croce Co. . . . .$4.

Iron-on transfer, Bart on skateboard, 1991. Gaffney. Australia. 10-by-7½-inch. Sealed. . . . .$5-$10.

Iron-on transfer, Ramada, Bart, 1994. Hotel chain promotional. Includes two transfers of Bart's face — one 4 inches and one 2 inches in diameter. Sealed. . . . .$1-$4.

Iron-on transfer, Ramada, family, 1994. Sheet includes two iron-on transfers showing the Simpsons family dressed for summer. Sealed. . . . .$1-$4.

Oval adhesive sticker, Bart, "Eat my shorts," 1990. 6-by-4-inches. . . . .$2.

Oval adhesive sticker, Bart, "I'm Bart Simpson. Who the hell are you?" 1990. 6-by-4-inches. . . . .$2.

Oval adhesive sticker, Bart, "Underachiever — and proud of it, man!" 1990. 6-by-4-inches. $2.

Oval adhesive sticker, Bartman, "Watch it, dude," 1990. 6-by-4-inches. . . . . . .$2.

Oval adhesive sticker, family dancing, "No problemo!!!" 1990. 6-by-4-inches. . . . .$2.

Oval adhesive sticker, The Simpsons, 1990. Family posing. 6-by-4-inches. . . . .$2.

Puffy stick-ons, 1990. Diamond Publishing Inc. 8-by-3½ inch sheet, with 10 raised stickers. Sealed. $3-$5.

Sticker activity book, "Samoleky," 1994. Kralicek. Czech Republic. 12-page soft-cover. 4½-by-3¼ inches. Four pages of puzzles and peel-off stickers. . . . .$12.

Simpsons stickers, 1993. Gibson. Four-sheet pack with nine stickers per sheet. Each features head shot of a Simpson character. Sealed. . . . . .$2-$5.

Sticker sheet, "Simpsonovi," 1994. Twentieth Century Fox Merchandising Prague. Czech Republic. 6-by-6-inch sheet with 11 peel-off stickers of Simpsons characters. . . . .$10.

Sticker Activity Album Stickers five-pack, 1990. Diamond. Five packets of album stickers with six stickers per pack. Accessories for Sticker Activity Album. Bagged. . . .$2-$4.

Sticker zone, 1997. American Greetings. Two-sheet pack with 20 stickers per sheet. Sealed. .$1-$2.

Stickers, Valentine, 1998. American Greetings. 4-sheet pack with nine stickers per sheet. Sealed. . . . .$1-$2.

Vinyl decals for bicycles and tricycles, 1990. Randor. Six decals per sheet. Sealed. . . . . . .$1-$3

Simpsons Sticker Zone pack, 1997, American Greetings. Most of the stickers feature an individual shot of a Simpsons family member.

Buttons and pins

1½-inch buttons, several variations, 1990. Button-Up. Metal base. Variations include: Bartman, Bart, the family, and "Happy Holidays." . . . .$1 each.

1½-inch buttons, 1989. Button-Up. White plastic backing. Variations include family, Homer, Bart. . . . .$2 each.

1⅜-inch Bongo promo buttons, 1997. Bongo Comics. Several characters, including Apu "Employee of the Year," Homer "Honorary Member, Sacred Order of the Stonecutters," Grampa "The Fighting Hellfish Platoon Mascot," and Roswell "The Roswell Incident, 1947-1997." . . . .$4 each.

3-inch promo button, Bart, "What's shakin', man?" 1990. Fox network. On Bart's blue shirt is a Fox logo. . . . .$5.

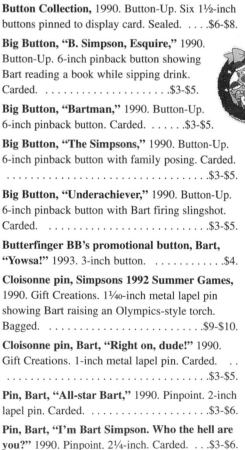

Button Collection, 1990. Button-Up. Six 1½-inch buttons pinned to display card. Sealed. . . . .$6-$8.

Big Button, "B. Simpson, Esquire," 1990. Button-Up. 6-inch pinback button showing Bart reading a book while sipping drink. Carded. . . . .$3-$5.

Big Button, "Bartman," 1990. Button-Up. 6-inch pinback button. Carded. . . . . . .$3-$5.

Big Button, "The Simpsons," 1990. Button-Up. 6-inch pinback button with family posing. Carded. . . . .$3-$5.

Big Button, "Underachiever," 1990. Button-Up. 6-inch pinback button with Bart firing slingshot. Carded. . . . .$3-$5.

Butterfinger BB's promotional button, Bart, "Yowsa!" 1993. 3-inch button. . . . .$4.

Cloisonne pin, Simpsons 1992 Summer Games, 1990. Gift Creations. 1¹⁄₄₀-inch metal lapel pin showing Bart raising an Olympics-style torch. Bagged. . . . .$9-$10.

Cloisonne pin, Bart, "Right on, dude!" 1990. Gift Creations. 1-inch metal lapel pin. Carded. . . . .$3-$5.

Pin, Bart, "All-star Bart," 1990. Pinpoint. 2-inch lapel pin. Carded. . . . .$3-$6.

Pin, Bart, "I'm Bart Simpson. Who the hell are you?" 1990. Pinpoint. 2¼-inch. Carded. . . .$3-$6.

Pin, Bart, "Shh ... don't tell, man," 1990. Pinpoint. 2-inch lapel pin. Carded. . . . . . .$3-$6.

Pin, Bart, "War is hell, man!" 1990. Pinpoint. 2¼-inch lapel pin. Carded. . . . .$3-$6.

Pin, Bart, "Yo dudes!" 1990. Pinpoint. 1½-inch lapel pin. Carded. . . . .$3-$6.

Pin, Bartman, "Watch it, dude!" 1990. Pinpoint. 2¼-inch lapel pin. Carded. . . . .$3-$6.

Pin, family posing, 1990. Pinpoint. 2¾-inch lapel pin. Carded. . . . .$3-$6.

Pin, holiday wreath, 1990. Pinpoint. 5-inch button in shape of wreath with family inside. Carded. . . . .$3-$7.

Ramada promotional button, Bart with sun visor, 1994. 3-inch button promoting hotel's "Simpsons Summer Break." $4

Auto window suction cup hangers

Bart, "Aye carumba!" 1990. H&L Entertainment. 5-by-5-inch plastic sign with suction cup at one corner. . . . . .$3.

Bartman, "Bartman on board," 1990. H&L Entertainment. . . . .$3.

Bart in graduation cap, "Class of '91," 1990. H&L Entertainment. . . . .$3.

Bart in graduation cap, "Class of '93," 1990. H&L Entertainment. . . . .$3.

Bart, "Cool your jets, man!" 1990. H&L Entertainment. . . . .$3.

Bart surfboarding, "Cowabunga, man!" 1990. H&L Entertainment. . . . .$3.

Bart, "Don't have a cow, man!" 1990. H&L Entertainment. . . . .$3.

Simpsons automobile window hangers, 1990, H&L Entertainment. Modeled after the famous "Baby on Board" signs of the late 1980s.

Far right, Bart Simpson "War is hell, man!" pin and Bartman "Watch it, dude!" pin, 1990, Pinpoint.

Bongo Comics promotional buttons, 1997. A rare opportunity to find a diverse group of characters, including one for Bongo's spinoff comic, Roswell.

Right, center, Simpsons holiday wreath pin, 1990, Pinpoint. The company also manufactured a similar-looking wreath magnet.

Bart, "Eat my shorts, man!" 1990. H&L Entertainment. . . . . . $3.

Bart leaning on skateboard, "I'm Bart Simpson. Who the hell are you?" 1990. H&L Entertainment. . . . . $3.

Bart on skateboard, "Outta my way, man," 1990. H&L Entertainment. . . . . $3.

Bart giving peace sign, "Peace dude," 1990. H&L Entertainment. . . $3.

Bart, "Watch it, dude!" 1990. H&L Entertainment. $3.

Bart shouting, "Whoa momma!" 1990. H&L Entertainment. $3.

Bart with thumbs up, "Yo, dude!" 1990. H&L Entertainment. $3.

Homer angry, "All-American Dad," 1990. H&L Entertainment. $3.

Homer choking Bart, "Have you hugged your kid today?" 1990. H&L Entertainment. . . . . $3.

Homer driving kids, "Are we there yet?" 1990. H&L Entertainment. 5-by-5-inch diamond-shaped plastic sign with suction cup. . . . . $3.

Simpsons door-knob hangers, 1990, H&L Entertainment. All styles feature one side with Bart and the caption, "Do not disturb."

Door knob hangers

Bart next to broken vase, "I didn't do It. Nobody saw me do it. You can't prove anything!" 1990. H&L Entertainment. 9-by-4-inch plastic sign designed to hang from a door knob. This and all other hangers show Bart's head and "Do Not Disturb" on one side. . . . . $3.

Bart, "I need my own space, man!" 1990. H&L Entertainment. $3.

Bart, "Off limits, man!" 1990. H&L Entertainment. $3.

Bart, "Peace man," 1990. H&L Entertainment. . . $3.

Homer choking Bart, "Enter at your own risk," 1990. H&L Entertainment. . . . . $3.

Homer, "Leave me alone," 1990. H&L Entertainment. $3.

Simpsons "All-American Dad" and "Yo, dude!" automobile window hangers, 1990, H&L Entertainment. Note the suction cup on the top corners.

Wall placards (10½-by-8-inch)

Bart, "Don't have a cow, man!" 1990. H&L Entertainment. Plastic sign. . . $5.

Bart, "Eat my shorts, man!" 1990. H&L Entertainment. . . .$5.

Bart, "Radical Dude," 1990. H&L Entertainment. . . . .$5.

Family on sofa, "Home Sweet Home," 1990. H&L Entertainment. . . . .$5.

Wall placards (11-by-17-inch)

Bart, "Skateboard parking," 1990. H&L Entertainment. Plastic sign. . . . .$8.

Bart aiming slingshot, "Underachiever," 1990. H&L Entertainment. . . . .$8.

Bart, "Underachiever ... and proud of it, man," 1990. H&L Entertainment. . . . .$8.

Bartman, "Bartman," 1990. H&L Entertainment. . . . .$8.

Street signs

Bart on skateboard, "Dude Dr," 1990. H&L Entertainment. 18-by-4½-inch plastic. . . . . . .$5.

Bart, Lisa and Maggie on sofa, "Kids' Zone," 1990. H&L Entertainment. . . . .$5.

Bart on skateboard, "Radical Rd," 1990. H&L Entertainment. . . . .$5.

Homer choking Bart, "Simpson St," 1990. H&L Entertainment. . . . .$5.

Posters

Bart "Eat my shorts, man!" 1990. Western Graphics. 20-by-15-inch. Framed. . . . .$18.

Bart "I'm Bart Simpson. Who the hell are you?" 1990. Can-Am Global Trading Co. Canada. 20-by-15 inches. . . . . $10.

Bart "Underachiever," 1990. Western Graphics. 20-by-15-inch. Framed. . . . .$18.

Bart "Radical Dude," 1989. Western Graphics. 32-by-21-inch. Rolled and sealed. . . . . . .$5-$10.

Merchandise review

Just about anything called a "collectible" probably isn't rare or valuable. And that appears to hold true for the set of six **Simpsons collector plates** from the Franklin Mint.

Who says cheesy has to be cheap? Imagine plunking down $35 or so for each of six plates too delicate to casually display and so toxic you might get poisoned by eating off them.

Each Franklin Mint plate is eight inches in diameter and suitable for hanging or displaying. Each comes with a "custom-designed plate stand."

According to promotional literature, each plate "is a limited edition ... bearing an original design and crafted of fine porcelain, bordered and hand-numbered in 24-karat gold." Each plate also bears the stamped-on signature of Matt Groening — "adding greatly to its significance," the literature notes. (Forget the fact that virtually every piece of Simpsons merchandise includes Groening's stamped-on signature.)

Furthermore, the back of the plates warn: "A decorative accessory. Not to be used for food consumption. Pigments used for color may be toxic."

The artwork on the plates is actually kind of good. Fans will particularly like one plate titled "Family Therapy," inspired by a scene from the episode, "There's No Disgrace Like Home," where the Simpsons administer shock therapy to each other.

Manufacturing of the plates, the Franklin Mint notes, was limited to 24 firing days, although the company doesn't say how many it can produce in about three weeks. At last check, the plates were still available by calling the Franklin Mint (1-800-225-5836).

Simpsons collector plates, 1991-'93, Franklin Mint. Six styles: "Caroling with the Simpsons," "Family Therapy," "A Family for the '90's," "Lisa and Her Sax," "Maggie and the Bears," and "Three-Eyed Fish."

Bart "Stay out of my room, man!" 1990. Western Graphics. 22-by-65-inch. Rolled and sealed. . . . .$10-$20.

Bart, Maxell parody, 1995. OSP Publishing. 36-by-24-inch. Bart in front of TV set, being swept back by force. Rolled and sealed. . . . .$3-$5.

Bartman, "Watch it, dude!" 1990. Western Graphics. 32-by-21-inch. Rolled and sealed. . . . .$5-$10.

Bartman "Avenger of Evil," 1990. Western Graphics. 32-by-21-inch. Rolled and sealed. . . . .$5-$10.

Family, "Christmas Special Video," 1991. 26-by-38-inch. Promotional poster for Fox home video release. Rolled. . . . .$15.

Family, posing, "Remember ... as far as anyone knows, we're a nice, normal family," 1990. Western Graphics. 32-by-21-inch. Rolled and sealed. . . . .$8-$12.

Family at window, "Let us out," 1997. OSP Publishing. 35-by-24-inch. Rolled and sealed. . . . .$3-$5.

Family, on sofa, 1997. OSP Publishing. 35-by-24-inch. Rolled and sealed. . . . .$3-$5.

Homer, "Obsimpson" Obsession cologne parody, 1996. OSP Publishing. 36-by-24- inch. Homer lounges in undershorts. . . . .$3-$5.

Poster-making kit, 1996. Copywrite. Four 12-by-16-inch posters and six wax crayons. Designs are 1. Simpsons making faces, 2. Homer asleep at the nuclear plant, 3. A crowd shot of Simpsons characters, and 4. Simpsons trying to get a cat out of a tree. Boxed. . . . .$10-$15.

Simpsons Sing the Blues, 1990. 20-by-30-inch. Promotional poster for 1991 Geffen album. Design shows Simpsons characters singing and playing musical instruments. Rolled. . . . .$12.

Tombstone Pizza "Achieving Bartitude," 1994. Tombstone Pizza. 24-by-36-inch. Six scenes with Bart's advice on living well. Rolled. . . . .$20.

Collector plates

"A Family for the '90's," 1991. Franklin Mint. 8-inch-diameter porcelain, bordered and hand-numbered in 24-karat gold. The Simpsons on the sofa watching TV. Boxed. . . . .$25-$35.

"Caroling with the Simpsons," 1991. Franklin Mint. The Simpsons sing in front of a Christmas tree. Boxed. . . . .$25-$35.

"Family Therapy," 1992. Franklin Mint. The Simpsons give each other electrical shocks at the office of Dr. Monroe. Boxed. . . . .$25-$35.

"Maggie and the Bears," 1992. Franklin Mint. Maggie is inside a cave with four bears. Boxed. . . . .$25-$35.

"Three-Eyed Fish," 1992. Franklin Mint. Marge serves Mr. Burns a three-eyed fish at dinner. Boxed. . . . .$25-$35.

"Lisa and Her Sax," 1993. Franklin Mint. Lisa plays saxophone with Bleeding Gums Murphy. Boxed. . . . .$25-$35.

Other

1991 Fun Calendar, 1991. Pantheon. Sealed. . . . .$5-$12.

1992 Fun Calendar, 1992. Sealed. . . . . . .$5-$12.

1993 Fun Calendar, 1993. Sealed. . . . . . .$5-$12.

1994 Fun Calendar, 1994. Sealed. . . . . . .$5-$12.

1995 Fun Calendar, 1995. Sealed. . . . . . .$5-$12.
(Note: There were no Simpsons calendars in the U.S. for 1996 or 1997.

1998 Fun Calendar, 1997. Danilo Printing. U.K. Sealed. . . . .$10-$15.

1999 Fun Calendar, 1998. Harper Collins. Sealed. . . . .$5-$12.

2000 "Another Are We There Yet?" Calendar, 1999. Harper Collins. Sealed. . . . .$10-$15.

Air freshener, Bart figurine, 1997. Custom Accessories Europe. 3-inch figurine showing Bart leaning on skateboard. Self-adhesive base. Carded. . . . .$5-$7.

Air freshener, Homer figurine, 1997. Custom Accessories Europe. 4-inch figurine showing Homer slapping head. Self-adhesive base. Carded. . . . .$5-$7.

Air freshener, Lisa figurine, 1997. Custom Accessories Europe. 3-inch figurine showing Lisa playing saxophone. Self-adhesive base. Carded. . $5-$7.

Air freshener, Marge figurine, 1997. Custom Accessories Europe. 4-1/2-inch figurine reminiscent of famous Marilyn Monroe with dress flying up. Self-adhesive base. Carded. . . . .$5-$7.

Automobile air freshener, Homer choking Bart, 1990. Medo. 4-by-3-inch scented card that hangs from a string. Sealed. . . . .$1-$4.

Automobile air freshener, family, "Are we there yet?" 1990. Medo. Sealed. . . . .$1-$4.

Automobile air freshener, Bart, "Eat my shorts," 1990. Medo. Sealed. . . . .$1-$4.

Automobile air freshener, Bart, "Enjoy the view, man!" 1990. Medo. Sealed. . . . .$1-$4.

Automobile air freshener, Bart, "In the hoop, man!" 1990. Medo. Sealed. . . . . $1-$4.

Automobile sun shade, family, "Honk if you love the Simpsons!" 1990. Roll-down shade suitable for blocking sunlight through a side window. . . . $10.

Hang Arounds wind sock, Bart, 1990. Spectra Star. 14-inch hollow cloth shaped like Bart. Boxed. . . . .$5-$20.

Holiday wreath magnet, 1990. Pinpoint. 5-inch pin in shape of wreath with Simpsons in the middle. Carded. . . . .$3-$7.

License plate holder, Bart,

Simpsons automobile air fresheners, 1990, Medo. 4-by-3-inch scented cards that hang from a string.

"Don't have a cow, man!" 1990. NJ Croce Co. 12-inch-wide white plastic. . . . .$5.

License plate holder, Bart, "Watch it, dude!" 1990. NJ Croce Co. 12-inch-wide white plastic. . . . .$5.

License plate holder, Bart, "Yo, dude!" 1990. NJ Croce Co. 12-inch-wide white plastic. . . . .$5.

Magnet, ceramic, Bart, "No way, man!" 1990. One of the Bunch. 2-inch-square. Carded. .$2-$5.

Magnet, ceramic, Homer, "Come back here, you little —," 1990. One of the Bunch. 2-inch-square. Carded. . . . .$2-$5.

Magnet, ceramic, Homer nuclear, 1990. Presents. 2½-by-2-inch ceramic decoration with magnet on back. Bagged. . . . .$2-$3.

Magnet, ceramic, Marge, 1990. Presents. 2½-by-2-inch ceramic decoration with magnet on back. Marge pictured with what looks like green Jello. Bagged. . . . .$3.

Magnet, Bart, making face, 1997. Vivid

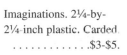
Nuclear glow Homer Simpson ceramic magnet, 1990, Presents.

Imaginations. 2¼-by-2¼-inch plastic. Carded. . . . .$3-$5.

Magnet, Bart and Homer, 1997. Vivid Imaginations. 3-by-1½-inch plastic. Bart and Homer stretched out in underwear watching TV. Carded. . . . . . .$3-$5.

Marge Simpson carrying food ceramic magnet, 1990, Presents.

Standee, Bart with skateboard, "Yo, man!" 1990. Starmakers. 16-inch cardboard cutout. Sealed. . . . .$2-$5.

Standee, family, 1990. Starmakers. 16-inch cardboard cutout. Sealed. . . . .$2-$4.

Standee, Marge/Homer hugging, 1990. Starmakers. 16-inch cardboard cutout. Sealed. . . . .$1-$4.

Wall banner, Bart, "Eat my shorts, man!" 1990. Coastal Concepts. 24-by-15-inch felt-like banner. Carded. . . . .$10-$15.

Wall banner, Bart, "I'm Bart Simpson. Who the hell are you?"

Simpsons automobile air fresheners, 1990. Two Bart styles: "Enjoy the view, man!" and "Eat my shorts."

1990. Coastal Concepts. 24-by-15-inch felt-like banner. Carded.   . . . .$10-$15.

Wall banner, Bartman, "Watch it, dude!" 1990. Coastal Concepts. 24-by-15-inch felt-like banner. Carded. . . . . . .$10-$15.

Wall banner, Homer, "Atomic Dad," 1990. Coastal Concepts. 24-by-15-inch felt-like banner shaped like home plate. Carded. . . . .
. . . .$10-$15.

Wall clock, family posing, 3-D, 1998. Wesco. 9½-inch diameter plastic cloth with raised images of Simpsons. Battery-operated. Boxed.   . . . .$15-$25.

Wall clock, family posing, 1990. JPI. 11-inch-diameter oval clock. Battery-operated. . . . .$20-$35.

Wall clock, Bart, 1997. Wesco. U.K. 10-inch-diameter circular clock shows the top half of Bart's head. Battery-operated. . . . .$10-$25.

Wall clock, Homer, "D'Oh!" 1997. Wesco. U.K. 10-inch-diameter clock showing Homer slapping his head. Battery-operated.   . . . .$10-$25.

Word magnets, 1996. Fridge Fun. Three magnetic vinyl sheets cut slightly so they can be broken into tiny rectangles with words on them. Boxed.   . . . .$3-$10.

Simpsons cardboard standee, 1990, Starmakers. A decorative item, approximately 16 inches high.

Bartman wall banner, 1990, Coastal Concepts. Original display card shows Bart saying, "They're the coolest, man!"

Simpsons 3-D wall clock, 1998, Wesco. U.K. This battery-operated clock features raised images of the family.

Bart Simpson "Write it down, man!" Write 'N Wipe memo board, 1990, Rose Art. 11-by-14-inch plastic with marker pen and sticker hangers.

Homer Simpson wall banner, 1990, Coastal Concepts. 24-by-15-inch felt-like material. Display card shows Bart saying, "They're the coolest, man!"

Simpsons bumper stickers, 1990, NJ Croce Co.

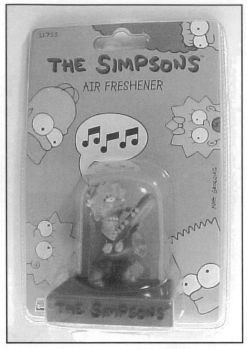

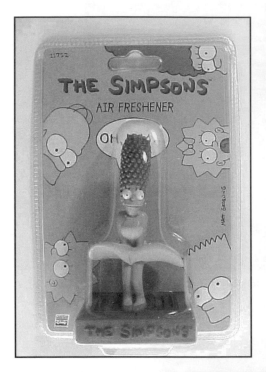

Bart, Homer, Lisa and Marge figurine air fresheners, 1997, Custom Accessories Europe. U.K. 3-to-4-inch figurines with self-adhesive base for mounting on car dash or other places.

Simpsons Ice Capades pennant, 1990. 28-inch-long
Felt-like promotional banner for ice show featuring
"The Simpsons."

Bart Simpson standee, 1990,
Starmakers. 16-inch cardboard
cutout.

Simpsons vinyl decals for bicycles and tricycles,
1990, Randor. Six styles: the family together,
Homer with fishing gear, Marge dancing, Maggie
alone, Lisa alone and Bart with slingshot.

Bart Simpson "Radical Dude" Big Button, 1990, Button-Up. 6-inch-diameter pinback button.

Homer Simpson wall clock, 1997, Wesco. UK. 10-inch-diameter. Pictured sealed in original cardboard display box.

Simpsons cork bulletin board, 1990, Rose Art. 22-by-16-inch.

Talking Homer Simpson alarm clock, 1998, Wesco. 10-inch-high. Wakes sleepers with five sayings: "Mmmm donuts ... Is there nothing they can't do?", "Donuts of the world, beware. It's judgment day!", "Marge, is there such a thing as a cake fairy?", "Awww, you deserve a sleep in. Go ahead and push the little snooze button" and "But I got up yesterday!"

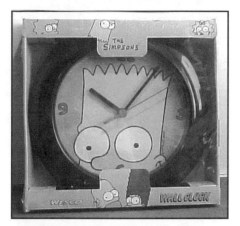

Bart Simpson wall clock, 1997, Wesco. U.K. 10-inch-diameter. Requires one AA battery.

Bart Simpson "Underachiever" cork bulletin board, 1990, Rose Art. 22-by-16-inch.

Ramada button, 1994. 3-inch-diameter pinback button for the hotel chain's promotion. Bart Simpson Butterfinger BB's button, 1993. 3-inch-diameter pinback button for the candymaker. Simpsons "Happy Holidays" buttons, 1990, Button-Up. 1½-inch-diameter pinback buttons, with Bart saying "Bah, humbug!" and Marge's hair in Christmas decorations.

Fridge magnets, 1997, Vivid Imaginations. U.K. Each is about 2 to 3 inches long. From left, Marge and Homer hugging, Homer sleeping on the sofa, Bart making a face, and Homer stretched on the sofa.

Valentine's stickers, 1998, American Greetings. 4-sheet pack with nine stickers per sheet. In the late 1990s, American Greetings became a major licensee of Simpsons merchandise.

Puffy Stick-Ons, 1990, Diamond Publishing. The company produced numerous variations of its puffy stickers, with this packet containing several styles. Each sticker has a cushion-like texture.

14 School and writing

Bookmarks

Bart PVC, 1990. Button-Up. 4-inch Bart-shaped figure that is flat from the chest down so it can fit inside a book as a marker. Bagged. . . . .$3-$5.

Bart, "Don't have a cow, man!" 1990. Legends of Entertainment. 5-inch plastic. . . . .$3.

Bart, "Fun has a name and it's Bartholomew J. Simpson," 1990. Legends of Entertainment. 5-inch plastic. . . . .$3.

Bart, "Outta my way, man!" 1990. Legends of Entertainment. 5-inch plastic. . . . .$3.

Family "Read man," 1990. American Library Association. 6-by-3-inch cardboard showing family on a sofa, all reading. . . . .$4.

Family posing, 1990. Legends of Entertainment. 5-inch plastic. . . . .$3.

Maggie, "Suck, suck, suck," 1990. Legends of Entertainment. 5-inch plastic. . . . .$3.

Krusty the Clown, "I didn't do it," 1992. O.S.P. Publishing. 5-inch plastic. . . . .$3.

Itchy and Scratchy, eating spaghetti, 1992. O.S.P. Publishing. 5-inch plastic. Cat is eating spaghetti as his head is blown loose from his body. Mouse is standing below with a smile and a lit bomb. . . . .$3.

Itchy and Scratchy, electrocution, 1992. O.S.P. Publishing. 5-inch plastic. Cat is getting electrocuted as he sticks a screwdriver into a toaster that the mouse plugged in. . . .$3.

Itchy and Scratchy, time bombs, 1992. O.S.P. Publishing.

5-inch plastic. Cat and mouse visible above lit time bombs. . . . .$3.

Simpsons plastic bookmarks, 1990, Legends of Entertainment. Three styles: "Fun has a name," "Family posing" and "Don't have a cow, man!"

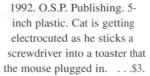

Simpsons address books, 1990, Legends of Entertainment. Three styles: Maggie, Marge and Homer.

"Nuclear messages!" Simpsons Write 'N Wipe message board, 1990, Rose Art. 11-by-14-inch plastic board with marker that wipes clean.

Write 'N Wipe memo boards

Bart, 11-by-14-inch, "Write it down, man!" 1990. Rose Art. Includes marker pen and stick-on hangers. Sealed. . . . .$5-$10.

Family, 11-by-14-inch, "Nuclear messages!" 1990. Rose Art. Includes marker pen and stick-on hangers. Sealed.$5- . . . .$10.

Lisa playing saxophone, 11-by-14-inch, "Notes!" 1990. Rose Art. Includes marker pen and stick-on hangers. Sealed. . . . .$5-$10.

Bart, 7-by-5-inch, "Write it down, man!" 1990. Rose Art. Sealed. . . . .$2-$7.

Family, 7-by-5-inch, 1990. Rose Art. Sealed. . . . .$2-$7.

Lisa, 7-by-5-inch, playing saxophone, 1990. Rose Art. Sealed. . . . .$2-$7.

Lisa Simpson saxophone Write 'N Wipe message board, 1990, Rose Art. Wouldn't this 11-by-14-inch board be perfect for musical notes?

Stationery

Address book, Homer, "Why you little —!" 1990. Legends of Entertainment. 4-by-3-inch white plastic holding about 50 pages. Bagged. $3- . . . .$5.

Address book, Marge, "Thank you, it's my specialty," 1990. Legends of Entertainment. 4-by-3-

Merchandise review

A sleeper find among Simpsons merchandise is the **Screenies computer screen frame**, a decorative item to stick around a video monitor.

This 1994 product is full of cleverness and comic detail.

The frame features a variety of computer-related humor, based on the theme of the Simpsons traveling the "information superhighway." There is the "SCSI port docking station," a street sign called "Disk Drive," and Bart leaning against a gasoline pump that reads, "Happy modeming." There is also a sign for the "Memory Lane Motel" and a billboard for "Satin spread sheets."

How cool when a manufacturer does something more than slap a few images and catch phrases on Simpsons merchandise.

Simpsons spiral-bound memo pads, 1990, Legends of Entertainment. 4-by-4½-inch pads featuring Bartman and the Simpsons family.

inch white plastic holding about 50 pages. Bagged. . . . .$3-$5.

Address book, Maggie, "Suck, suck, suck," 1990. Legends of Entertainment. 4-by-3-inch white plastic holding about 50 pages. Bagged. . . . .$3-$5.

Diary, Maggie, "Baddest sucker in town," 1990. Legends of Entertainment. 5-by-7-inch with white plastic slip cover. Includes tiny padlock and key. . . . .$10.

Filler tablet, Bart "No class today!" 1990. Legends of Entertainment. 10½-by-8-inch notebook with 30 sheets. . . . .$7.

Filler tablet, Maggie, "Suck, suck, suck," 1990. Legends of Entertainment. 10½-by-8-inch notebook with 30 sheets. . . . .$7.

Memo book, wire bound, Bart "Radical dude!" 1990. Legends of Entertainment. 6-by-4-inch spiral bound with 50 sheets. . . . .$5.

Memo book, wire bound, family, "America's most nuclear family," 1990. Legends of Entertainment. 6-by-4-inch spiral bound with 50 sheets. . . . .$5.

Memo book, wire bound, Homer "World's Angriest Dad," 1990. Legends of Entertainment. 6-by-4-inch spiral bound with 50 sheets. . . . .$5.

Memo book, wire bound, Lisa "Overachiever," 1990. Legends of Entertainment. 6-by-4-inch spiral bound with 50 sheets. . . . .$5.

Memo book, wire bound, Maggie "Baddest sucker in town," 1990. Legends of Entertainment. 6-by-4-inch spiral bound with 50 sheets. . . . .$5.

Memo book, wire bound, Marge "World's best cook," 1990. Legends of Entertainment. 6-by-4-inch spiral bound with 50 sheets. . . . .$5.

Memo book, wire bound and die-cut, Bartman, 1990. Legends of Entertainment. 4-by-4½-inch

spiral bound with 50 sheets. . . . .$5.

Memo book, wire bound and die-cut, family, 1990. Legends of Entertainment. 4-by-4½-inch spiral bound with 50 sheets. Pad cut into shape of design. Pages feature same design printed lightly over each sheet. . . . .$5.

Memo pad, Bart, "Don't have a cow, man!" 1989. Legends of Entertainment. 6-by-4½-inch pad of paper with die-cut top. Sealed. . . . .$5-$8.

Memo pad, Bart, "Eat my shorts, man!" 1990. Legends of Entertainment. 6-by-4½-inch pad of white paper with die-cut top. Sealed. . . . . .$5-$8.

Memo pad, Bartman, "Watch it, dude," 1990. Legends of Entertainment. 6-by-4½-inch pad of white paper with die-cut top. Sealed. . . . . .$5-$8.

Memo pad, family, 1990. Legends of Entertainment. 6-by-4½-inch pad of white paper with die-cut top. Sealed. . . . .$5-$8.

Memo pad, Maggie, 1990. Legends of Entertainment. 6-by-4½-inch pad of white paper with die-cut top. Sealed. . . . .$5-$8.

Stationery diary/address book set, Bart, "Don't have a cow, man," 1990, Legends of Entertainment. Includes diary with lock, a 3-by-4-inch address book, and two pencils. Boxed. . . . .$7-$12.

Stationery pack, 1990. Legends of Entertainment. Includes address book, two pencils, memo book, ruler, eraser and pencil sharpener. Carded. . . . .$4-$12.

Stationery Value Pack, 1990. Legends of Entertainment. Clear vinyl 6-by-8-inch pouch that contains two spiral-bound 3-by-5-inch memo pads, 6-inch plastic ruler, circular eraser and pencil. . . . .$12.

Theme book, wire bound, Bart "Eat my shorts, man!" 1990. Legends of Entertainment. 10½-by-8-inch notebook with 50 sheets of paper. . . . .$7.

Theme book, wire bound, family, "America's most nuclear family," 1990. Legends of Entertainment. 10-1/2-by-8-inch notebook with 50 sheets of paper. . . . .$7.

Other

1999 Quotable Homer Desktop Calendar, 1998, Harper Collins. 365-day desktop calendar, designed by Bongo Entertainment. Features Homer quotations from the series and a trivia game. Boxed. . . . .$10-$20.

2000 Quotable Bart Desktop Calendar, 1999.

Bart Simpson soft-vinyl lunch box with bottle, 1990, Thermos. On the bottle, Bart writes on the chalk board: "I will not juggle food in the cafeteria."

Homer and Bart Simpson backpack, 1990, Imaginings. Vinyl design shows Homer saying, "Pardon my French" and "Come back here you little —!" Bart is saying, "Whoa mama!"

Harper Collins. 366-day desktop calendar, designed by Bongo. Features Bart's chalkboard promises, telephone pranks and notable quotables. Boxed. . . . .$8-$13.

Back pack, Bart and Lisa, 1990. Imaginings. Vinyl 18-inch-long with black straps. Tagged and bagged. . . . .$12-$35.

Back pack, Homer and Bart, 1990. Imaginings. Vinyl 18-inch-long carry-all with black straps. Tagged and bagged. . . . .$12-$35.

Binder, 2-ring, Homer, "D'oh," 1996. Australia. 9½-by-12-inch hard binder with two snap-open rings. Inside are blank class schedule and address grids. . . . .$7.

Book covers, three-pack, 1990. Legends of Entertainment. 13¼-by-22-inch. Three styles: "Eat my shorts, man!," "Don't have a cow, man!" and "No class today!" Sealed. . . . .$1.50-$4.

Chalk, Bart, 1990. Noteworthy. 4-inch figural Bart that's dustless chalk. For chalkboards and sidewalks. Carded. . . . .$3-$8.

Chalk, Church's Chicken promo, 1996. 4-inch-long chalk. Three variations: Homer, Marge and Bart. Sealed. . . . .$3.

Computer screen frame, 1994. Screenies. 12-by-16-inch decorative cardboard frame that fits around a computer monitor. Sealed. . . . . .$7-$15.

Cork bulletin board, Bart "Underachiever," 1990. Rose Art. 22-by-16-inch. Sealed. . .$5-$10.

Cork bulletin board, family posing, 1990. Rose Art. 22-by-16-inch. Sealed. . . . .$5-$10.

Eraser, Bart, 1990. Street Kids. 3½-inch eraser shaped like Bart. Variations: Red shirt, orange shirt, light-blue shirt and dark-blue shirt. Carded. . . . .$2-$6.

Eraser, Bart, 1996. Marbig Rexel. Australia. 2½-inch. Carded. . . . .$2-$5.

Glue stick, Bart, 1996. Marbig Rexel Pty. Ltd. Australia. 4-inch-high tube. Carded. . .$5-$15.

Lunch box, hard plastic, with insulated bottle, 1990. Thermos. Red hard-plastic box with sticker nearly covering one side. Sticker shows

Bart juggling food. Bottle is white with red cap. On the bottle, Bart writes on chalk board: "I will not juggle food in the cafeteria." Tagged. . . .$15 without Thermos bottle, $25 with Thermos bottle.

Lunch box, soft vinyl, "Time for refueling, man," with insulated bottle, 1990. Thermos. Red soft-vinyl box shows Bart on one side holding a carton of milk and other food. White bottle, 1991, with red cap and design. Variations include Bart holding up a bottle and Bart at chalk board. Tagged. . . . .$20 without Thermos bottle, $30 with Thermos bottle.

Homer Simpson cap, mug and mouse pad promoting 1998 ad campaign by Intel, maker of computer processors. The design shows Homer's head with "Intel Inside" stamped on the back of it.

Mouse pad, Bart, "Click on someone your own size, man!" 1995. Office Gear. 9 inches wide. Sealed. . . . .$3-$12.

Simpsons mouse pad promoting the 1995 "Who Shot Mr. Burns?" contest from long-distance phone service 1-800-COLLECT.

Bart Simpson hard-vinyl lunch box with bottle, 1990, Thermos. Note the bottle has a similar design to one packaged with the soft-vinyl lunch box.

Mouse pad, Homer, asleep at nuclear plant, 1995. Office Gear. 9-inch-wide. Sealed. . . . .
. . . .$3-$12.

Mouse pad, Homer, "Intel Inside," 1998. Intel. 7-by-7½-inch. Blue with design showing back of Homer's head with "Intel Inside" stamped on it. . . . .$10.

Simpsons pencil case, 1996, Hungry Jack's. Australia. Promotional item from the fast-food restaurant chain.

Mouse pad, "Who Shot Mr. Burns?" 1995. Photo Pad. 7-by-7½-inch. Promotional item for Simpsons Mystery Sweepstakes from 1-800-COLLECT. Pad shows perspective of fallen Mr. Burns looking between his legs at Homer and others. . . . . .$15.

Notebook folder, Bart, "Eat my shorts, man!" 1989. Legends of Entertainment. Double pockets inside. . . . .$4.

Notebook folder, Bart, "No class today!" 1989. Legends of Entertainment. Double pockets inside.
. . . .$4.

Notebook folder, family in car, 1997. Class Acts. Double pockets inside. Logos of Sun Coast, Sam Goody, Media Play, Musicland and On-Cue stores on back. . . . .$2.

Notebook folder, Homer choking Bart, 1989. Legends of Entertainment. Double pockets inside.
. . . .$4.

Notebook folder, Maggie on skateboard, 1989. Legends of Entertainment. Double pockets inside.
. . . .$4.

Notebook folder, nuclear family, 1989. Legends of Entertainment. Double pockets inside. . . . .$4.

Pen, Bart with slingshot, 1991. 5½-inch-long with blue ink. Snap-on top with pocket clip. Carded. . . . .$4-8.

Pen, ballpoint, Bart (four designs), 1997. Penline MonAmi. Australia. 5¼-inch-long. Variations: Bart with basketball, Bart with arms outstretched, Bart in front of stadium. Black ink. Carded. . . . .$3-7.

Pen, ballpoint, Marge and Homer in bathtub, 1997. Penline MonAmi. Australia. 5¼-inch-long. Carded. . . . .$3-$7.

Pen, roller, Bart (four designs), 1995. MonAmi. Australia. 5½-inch-long "roller pen." Variations: Bart surfing, Bart as Cupid, one with arms outstretched and one in front of a stadium. All have black ink, except for stadium one, which has blue ink. Carded. . . . .$3-$7.

Pen, roller, Marge with plate of food, 1995. MonAmi. Australia. 5½ inches long. Black ink. Carded. . . . .$3-$7.

Pen, roller, Marge and Homer in tub, 1995. MonAmi. 5½ inches long. Black ink. Carded. . . .
. . . .$3-$7.

Pencil case, Hungry Jacks, 1996. Australia. 8½-by-2½-inch. Metal with hinges. Design shows heads of Simpsons family. . . . .$10.

Pencil pack, Bart, 1990. Noteworthy. Four white pencils showing Bart in various poses. Carded. . .
. . . .$2-$5.

Pencil topper, Bart, 1997. Vivid Imaginations. U.K. 7-inch pencil with 2½-inch figure of Bart on a skateboard. Carded. . . . .$3-$8.

Pencil topper, Homer, 1997. Vivid Imaginations. U.K. 7-inch pencil with 3-inch figure of Homer. Carded. . . . .$3-$8.

School kit, Bart and Lisa, 1990. Imaginings. Zippered pouch with ruler, eraser and pencil sharpener. Design on pouch shows Bart tossing a paper airplane. Sealed. . . . .$3-$10.

School supplies holder, Bart, Lisa and Maggie, 1991. Danesa. Spain. 9½-by-6-inch translucent plastic pouch with zipper on one side and holes on the other for putting the holder into three-ring binder. . . . .$15.

School supplies holder, large, Bart, 1996. Australia. 13-inch-by-6½-inch vinyl pouch with zipper. Design shows Bart booting soccer ball, Bart hitting it with his head, and Bart lightly kicking it. Sealed. . . . .$5-$10.

School supplies holder, small, Bart, 1996. Australia. 8-by-5 inch. Sealed. . . . .$3-$8.

Homer Simpson school-supplies holder, 1996. Australia. Design is the same on both sides of the pouch.

School supplies holder, large, Homer, 1996. Australia. 13-by-6½-inch vinyl pouch with zipper. Design shows Homer slapping his head, Homer smiling and Homer tossing what looks like popcorn into his mouth. Sealed. . . . .$5-$10.

School supplies holder, small, Homer, 1996. 8-by-5-inch. Sealed. . . . .$3-$8.

Study kit, Bart kicking soccer ball, 1996. Pancake Press. Australia. Includes 9-by-4-inch blue zippered pouch. Includes 6-inch ruler, pencil sharpener and eraser. Sealed. . . . .$5-$15.

Wrist rest, Bart's head, 1995. Fellows. 2-foot-long pad for computer users. Sealed. . . . .$3-$12.

Wrist rest, Homer at nuclear plant, 1995. Fellows. 2 foot-long pad for computer users. Sealed. . . . .$3-$12.

Homer Simpson 3-ring binder, 1996. Australia. 9½-by-12-inch hard-cover binder with two snap-open rings. Includes grids for class schedule, names, addresses and phone numbers.

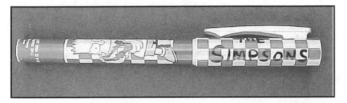

Bart Simpson ballpoint pen, 1991. 5½-inch blue-ink pen with snap-on top with pocket clip.

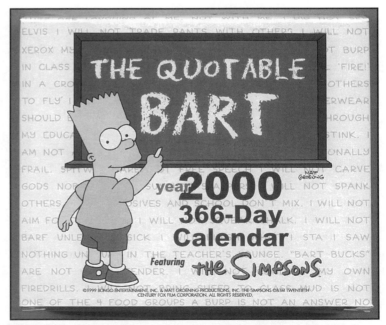

2000 Quotable Bart Desktop Calendar, 1999, Harper Collins. This 366-day desktop calendar features Bart's "brilliant observations" on sibling rivalry, sports, the media and religion, as well as chalkboard sayings and telephone pranks.

Simpsons notebook folders, 1989, Legends of Entertainment. Approximately 9-by-12-inch, with two storage pockets inside each folder.

2000 Simpsons "Another Are We There Yet?" Calendar, 1999, Harper Collins. The 24-page calendar draws art from the 1998 book, "The Simpsons Guide to Springfield."

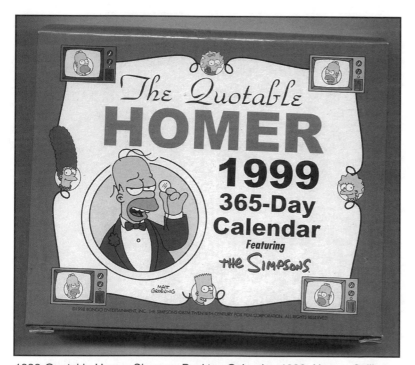

1999 Quotable Homer Simpson Desktop Calendar, 1998, Harper Collins. This 365-day desktop calendar is packed with screen shots from various episodes, accompanied by Homer's off-kilter insights and observations. There's also a built-in trivia game to guess the episode for that day's quotation and illustration.

15 Household goods

Kitchen accessories

Apron, kitchen gourmet, Marge "Her Supreme Momness," 1990. Innova. 21½-by-29½-inch. Sealed. . . . .$7-$12.

Apron, kitchen gourmet apron, Marge, "Come 'N' Get It," 1990. Innova. 21½-by-29½-inches. Sealed. . . . . . .$7-$12.

Apron, kitchen gourmet, Marge, "Who's Next?" 1990. Innova. 21½-by-29½-inch. Sealed. . . .$7-$12.

Apron, holiday gourmet, Marge, "Christmas Sugar Cookies," 1990. Innova. 21½-by-29½-inch. Includes recipe for sugar cookies. Sealed. . . . .$7-$12.

Apron, holiday gourmet, Marge, family around the Christmas tree, 1990. Innova. 21½-by-29½-inch. Sealed. . . . . . .$7-$12.

Bib, Baby Bart, 1992. Binky. Design shows Baby Bart using a spoon to splatter food. Carded. . . . .$2-$5.

Candy molds, 1990. Wilton. Clear plastic sheet with 7 candy molds — two of Bart, two of Lisa and one each of Homer, Marge and Maggie. Use with Wilton Candy Melts or similar product. Carded. . . . . . .$5-$7.

Cookie cutters, 1990. Wilton. Five shaped like the heads of Simpsons. Bagged. . . . . . .$5-$15.

Cookie jar, Bart, 1995. Treasure Craft. 14 inches high. Molded and painted to look like Bart munching on giant chocolate chip cookie. Bart's head forms the lid of jar. Boxed. . . . .$30-$50.

Cookie jar, Homer, 1995. Treasure Craft. 12 inches high. Molded and painted to look like Homer standing over a barrel-like cookie jar, with cookies stuffed into his mouth and the back of his blue pants. Boxed. . . . .$25-$55.

Lunch bags, Homer, "Kiss the chef," 1990. The Fern Group Limited. Canada. 25 bags. Sealed. . . . .$5-$15.

Placemat, family, Burger King, 1990. Burger King. 10-by-14-inch paper. Design shows Homer, Marge, Lisa and Bart alternately saying "Good drink!" "Good meat!" "C'mon!" "Let's eat!" . . . . ` . . . .$2.

Salt and pepper shakers, Bart and Lisa, 1997. Treasure Craft. Three-piece ceramic set, 3½ inches. Bart and Lisa in front of a TV set. Boxed. . . . .$20-$35.

Salt and pepper shakers, Homer, Marge and Maggie, 1997. Treasure Craft. Three-piece ceramic. 7 inches high. Homer, Marge and Maggie on a sofa. . . . .$25-$40.

Sip-a-roos box drink holder, 1990. Toymax. 4½-inch-high plastic. Holds disposable drink boxes. Carded. . . . .$5-$12.

Sun catcher, Bart with slingshot, "Eat my shorts," 1990. Global Express. Czech Republic. 8-inch-high plastic translucent cut-out that hangs in a window. . . . .$12.

Sun catcher, Bart, "Don't have a cow, man," 1990. Global Express. Czech Republic. 9-inch-high plastic translucent cut-out. . . . . .$12.

Sun catcher, Lisa, standing alone, 1991. Global Express. Czech Republic. 12-inch-high plastic translucent cut-out. . . . .$12.

Sun catcher, Maggie on scooter, 1990. Global Express. Czech Republic. 8-inch-high plastic translucent cut-out. . . . .$12.

Marge Simpson kitchen aprons, 1990, Innova. Three styles: "Christmas Sugar Cookies," "Her Supreme Momness" and "Come 'N' Get It."

Bart Simpson "Don't have a cow, man" sun catcher, 1990, Global Express. Czech Republic.

Lisa Simpson sun catcher, 1990, Global Express. Czech Republic.

Drinking utensils

Simpsons glasses, 1996, Nutella. Australia. 5-inch-high glasses originally sold as containers for chocolate spread.

Cup, plastic, KFC, Homer, 1993. Canada. 6½-inch-high plastic drinking cup showing Homer's face and Pepsi logo. . . . .$7.

Cup, paper, 7-Eleven "Who Shot Mr. Burns?" mug shots, 1995. Cup shows mug shots of nine suspects in the shooting of Mr. Burns. . . . .$5.

Cup, paper, 7-Eleven "Who Shot Mr. Burns?" Burns keeled over, 1995. Cup shows Burns' feet sticking up as anxious Simpsons characters look on. . . . .$5.

Cup, paper, 7-Eleven "Who Shot Mr. Burns?" suspect lineup, 1995. Cup shows Homer, Bart, Skinner, Smithers and Barney in a police lineup. . . . .$5.

Cup, paper, 7-Eleven "Who Shot Mr. Burns?" police chief, 1995. Cup shows chief of police looking at photos of several suspects. . . .$5.

Cup, plastic, Burger King "Bigfoot," 1990. 32-ounce. Bart on stilts meets Big Foot. . . . .$7.

Cup, plastic, Burger King "Bird-watching," 1990. 32-ounce. . . . . . .$7.

Cup, plastic, Burger King "Campfire," 1990. 32-ounce. Homer tries to start fire. . . . .$7.

Cup, plastic, Burger King "Nature show," 1990. 32-ounce. The family is watching TV in the woods as animals peer on. . . . .$7.

Cup, paper, Subway, 1997. Subway sandwich restaurants. 32-ounce. Yellow paper cup. Design shows Homer sucking up a large soda through a straw. . . . .$5.

Sipper cups, KFC (set of four), 1998. Kentucky Fried Chicken. Australia. Each has Simpsons design and figural topper featuring Simpsons. Each topper is 5 inches high and features a hole for 12-inch white plastic straws. Bagged. . . . .$3-$10 each.

Cup, Winchell's spill-proof, Homer, 1993. Winchell's doughnut shops. 5-inch-high white plastic with a red spill-proof lid. . . . .$5.

Glasses, Nutella, 1996. Nutella. Australia. 5-inch-high containers originally sold with chocolate spread.

Includes glass for each Simpson, Krusty the Clown, Sideshow Bob and Mr. Burns. .$10 each.

Mug, ceramic, Bart, "Don't have a cow, man!" 1990. One of the Bunch. 4-inch-high. . . . . . .$15.

Mug, ceramic, Bart, "Don't have a cow, man!" 1990. Presents. 4-inch-high. Inside the lip of the cup is Bart saying, "Well, maybe one more refill!" Boxed. . . . .$10-$20.

Mug, ceramic, Bart, "Peace Man," 1990. Presents. 4-inch-high. Inside the lip of the cup is peace symbol. Boxed. . . . .$10-$20.

Mug, ceramic, Bart, "Underachiever," 1990. One of the Bunch. 4-inch-high. . . . .$15.

Mug, ceramic, family, "Nuclear Family," 1990. Presents. 4-inch-high. Five heads of the Simpsons as spinning electrons. Inside the lip of the cup is fall-out shelter sign. . . . .$10-$20.

Mug, ceramic, family, 1990. One of the Bunch. 4-inch-high. The other side of the mug has the logo for "The Simpsons." . . . . .$15.

Mug, ceramic, Homer, "Atomic Dad," 1990. Presents. 4-inch-high. Inside the lip of the cup shows Homer's head with electrons around it. Boxed. . . . .$10-$20.

Mug, ceramic, Homer, "Intel Inside," 1998. Intel. 4-inch-high. Promotional for Intel's 1998 ad campaign. . . . .$8.

Simpsons paper cups from 1995's "Who Shot Mr. Burns?" promotion by 7-Eleven convenience stores. One cup shows mug shots of nine suspects; the other shows a fallen Burns.

Simpsons plastic cups, 1990, Burger King. 32-ounce plastic. Two designs: "Campfire" and "Bigfoot."

Simpsons sipper cups, 1998, KFC. Australia. Offered with plastic straw and tops shaped like the heads of Homer, Marge, Bart and Lisa.

Simpsons "Nature Show" plastic cup, 1990, Burger King. 32-ounce plastic.

Simpsons ceramic mugs, 1990, One of the Bunch. From left, Marge, Homer, Bart, Bart and the family. The reverse sides have a logo for "The Simpsons."

Simpsons frosty mug, 1997. Instructions on bottom: "Place mug upside-down in freezer compartment until liquid freezes." The mug keeps drinks cool for a long time.

Mug, ceramic, Homer, "Why you little —!" 1990. One of the Bunch. 4-inch-high. . . . . . .$15.

Mug, ceramic, Lisa, "Overachiever," 1990. Presents. 4-inch-high. Inside the lip of the mug is Lisa saying, "Phew!" Boxed. . . . . .$10-$20.

Mug, ceramic, Maggie "Baby Face," 1990. Presents. 4-inch-high. Inside the lip of the cup is the image of a pacifier. Boxed. . . . .$10-$20.

Mug, ceramic, Marge, "World's Best Cook," 1990. Presents. 4-inch-high. Inside the lip of the cup is Marge saying, "How 'bout a refill?" . . . .$10-$20.

Mug, ceramic, Marge, "Thank you, it's my specialty," 1990. One of the Bunch. 4-inch-high. . .$15.

Mug, frosty, family in convertible, 1997. 6-inch-high clear plastic. Sealed into mug is liquid that, when frozen, keeps drink cold. . . . .$8.

Mug, plastic, family posing. Betras Plastics. . . . .$5.

Mug, porcelain, Bart with arms folded. Thun Karlovasky Porcelan. Czech Republic. 4-inch-high. . . . .$20.

Mug, porcelain, Bart with bath towel. Thun Karlovasky Porcelan. Czech Republic. 4-inch-high. . . . .$20.

Mug, porcelain, Bart with arms folded. Thun Karlovasky Porcelan. Czech Republic. 4-inch-high. . . . .$20.

Mug, porcelain, Bart on skateboard. Thun Karlovasky Porcelan. Czech Republic. 4-inch-high. . . . .$20.

Mug, porcelain, Bart tossing a football. Thun Karlovasky Porcelan. Czech Republic. 4-inch-high. . . . .$20.

Mug, porcelain, Bart with arms folded. Thun Karlovasky Porcelan. Czech Republic. 4-inch-high. . . . .$20.

Mug, porcelain, Bart with umbrella. Thun Karlovasky Porcelan. Czech Republic. 4-inch-high. . . . .$20.

Mug, porcelain, Homer "Atomic Dad." Thun

Simpsons jug, 1996, Church's Chicken. Simpsons promotional items also included drawing chalk.

Bart Simpson chocolate egg with ceramic mug, 1998, Kinnerton. Australia.

Karlovasky Porcelan. Czech Republic. 4-inch-high. . . . .$20.

Mug, porcelain, Homer standing. Thun Karlovasky Porcelan. Czech Republic. 4-inch-high. . . . .$20.

Mug, porcelain, Lisa running. Thun Karlovasky Porcelan. Czech Republic. 4-inch-high. . . . .$20.

Mug, porcelain, Marge dancing. Thun Karlovasky Porcelan. Czech Republic. 4-inch-high. . . . .$20.

Jug, Church's Chicken, "Summer with the Simpsons," 1996. 9-inch-high, 5-inch-wide jug with two spouts, plastic straw and handle. Design shows Bart tossing beachball. . . . .$15.

Water bottle, Bart surfing, "Cowabunga, man!" 1990. Betras Plastics. 7-inch-high plastic orange bottle. . . . .$5.

Water bottle, family posing, 1990. Betras Plastics. 7-inch-high plastic. Shows family making bunny ears over each others' heads. . . . .$3.

Water bottle, family, posing, 1989. 7-inch-high plastic bottle shows family posing while making bunny ears over each others' heads. Other side shows family posing, with Bart aiming slingshot. . . . .$8.

Water bottle, Bart "Radical Dude!" Betras Plastics. 7-inch-high white plastic bottle. . .$5.

Water bottle, family and Bart, 1997. Headstart. Australia. 6-inch-high white and yellow plastic, with pop-up lid. . . . .$12.

Simpsons plastic water bottle, 1990, Betras Plastics. One of the company's numerous styles of Simpsons bottles.

Food and drink

Chocolate egg with ceramic mug, Bart, "Trust me. I'd never lie to you," 1998. Kinnerton. Australia. 65-gram hollow milk chocolate egg, wrapped in foil. Accompanied by 4-inch-high mug. Carded. . . . . $10-$15.

Chocolate shapes, 1997. St. Michael. Canada. Nine solid milk chocolates shaped like the Simpsons. Boxed. . . . . $5-$10.

Coco Pops cereal with free watch offer, 1997. Kellogg's. Australia. Includes offer for three limited edition Simpsons watches. (Offer expired.) Sealed. . . . . $3-$10.

Corn chips, CC's, 1997. The Smith's Snackfood Co. Australia. 50-gram bags. Corn chip packaging features Simpsons. Bart on two versions, Homer on two, and one each for Lisa, Mr. Burns, Marge and Krusty. Sealed. . . . . $2-$10 for each.

Coco Pops cereal with Simpsons watch offer, 1997, Kellogg's. Australia. Both the box's contents and the watch offer are now expired.

Simpsons CC's corn chips, 1997, The Smith's Snackfood Co. Australia. Homer appeared on several different packages. Some included a Simpsons 3-D puzzle piece.

Amurol Products. Sealed. . . . . . . $2-$6.

Gum, 40-stick pack, family on couch, 1990. Amurol Products. Sealed. . . . . $2-$6.

Gum, pouch, Bart "Gangway, Man!" 1990. Amurol Products. 2.10-oz. Sealed. . . . . $2-$6.

Gum, pouch, Bart "Right on, dude!" 1990. Amurol Products. 2.10-oz. Sealed. . . . . . $2-$6.

Gum, tube, Bart with slingshot, 1990, Amurol Products. 1.6-oz. Sealed. . . . . $2-$7.

Honey Smacks cereal with Bartman mask, 1997, Kellogg's. Australia. Cut-out mask offered on the back of the box.

Kit Kat chocolate bar with Simpsons promotion, 1997, Nestles. U.K. Packaging includes a now-expired offer for a Bart watch.

Honey Smacks cereal with Bartman mask, 1997. Kellogg's. Australia. 275-gram box with cut-out Bartman mask on back. Sealed. . . $3-$10.

Juice boxes, Orange A'Licious, 1991. Sweetripe Drinks. Canada. Three 8.45-fluid-ounce boxes of drink made from concentrate. . . . . $7-$15.

Kit Kat milk chocolate fingers, Simpsons, 1997. Nestles. U.K. Wrappers feature chance to win 20,000 pounds and Bart watch. (Offers expired.) Sealed. . . . . $3-$5.

Lollipop, chocolate Bart, 1997. St. Michael. U.K. 3½-inch Bart-shaped chocolate on a stick. Sealed. . . . . $1-$5.

Macaroni and cheese Fun Shapes, 1997. Kraft. Australia. Pasta shaped like Simpsons. Boxed. . . . . $2-$8.

Simpsons macaroni and cheese Fun Shapes, 1997, Kraft. Australia. Boxed pasta shaped like Homer, Bart and other characters.

Fruit Loops cereal with Simpsons Magic Motion card inside, 1997, Kellogg's. Australia. The box reads: "Watch the world's funniest family come to life simply by tilting the card up and down in your hands!"

Caramel corn, Bart on skateboard, 1992. Sabritas. Mexico. 50-gram bag. Sealed. . . . . . $1-$7.

Fruit Loops cereal with Magic Motion card inside, 1997. Kelloggs. Australia. Sealed. . . . . $3-$10.

Gingerbread, Bart, 1996. Great Australian Gingerbread Co. Australia. 6-by-3½-inch cookie in the shape of Bart's head. Sealed. . . . . . . $2-$10.

Gum, 40-stick pack, Bart surfing, 1990.

Bart Simpson caramel corn, 1992, Sabritas. Mexico. 50-gram bag.

Talking Bart Simpson alarm clock, 1991, Wesco. U.K. The company in 1998 produced a similar model showing Homer holding a donut.

Milk chocolates, boxed, 1997. Confection Concepts. New Zealand. 180-gram box contains 14 pieces shaped like Simpsons. Boxed. . . . .$5-$9.

Milk chocolates, Shrinkums, 1997. Confection Concepts. New Zealand. 150-gram bag contains 12 wrapped pieces shaped like Bart. Bagged. . . . .$5-$9.

Rice Bubbles cereal with Simpsons stickers set inside, 1997. Kellogg's. Australia. 800-gram box offering six sets of Simpsons stickers inside. 275-gram box doesn't have stickers, just game to find Bart among characters on the back. Sealed. . . . . . .$5-$10.

Bedroom

Alarm clock, Bart, blue, 1997. Wesco. U.K. 5-inch-high circular clock framed in blue plastic. Battery operated. Boxed. . . . . $12-$18.

Alarm clock, Bart, yellow, 1997. Wesco. U.K. 5-inch-high circular clock framed in yellow plastic. Battery operated. Boxed. . . . .$12-$18.

Alarm clock, talking Bart, 1991. Wesco. U.K. 9-inch figure of Bart holding red skateboard that features digital clock. Bart's voice wakes sleepers with, "Yo dude! Wake up and get out of bed" and "Hey, man! Aren't you out of bed yet?" Battery-operated. Boxed. . . . .$25-$50.

Alarm clock, talking Homer, 1998. Wesco. U.K. 10-inch figure of Homer holding a doughnut and a slice of cake that's a digital clock. Homer's voice wakes sleepers with, "Mmmm donuts ... Is there nothing they can't do?" "Donuts of the world, beware. It's judgment day!" "Marge, is there such a thing as a cake fairy?" "Awww, you deserve a sleep-in. Go ahead and push the little snooze button" and "But I got up yesterday!" Battery-operated. Boxed. . . . .$25-$50.

Alarm clock, talking radio, 1997. Wesco. U.K. 9-by-7-inch AM/FM clock radio modeled after Simpsons living room. Homer sleeps in his underwear on the sofa as Bart pours liquid on his face. Battery-operated. Boxed. . . . .$35-$50.

Comforter, 1990. Dreamstyle. Twin-size "coordinating comforter." Design shows Simpsons in various poses. Sealed. . . . .$10-$50.

Simpsons talking radio alarm clock, 1997, Wesco. U.K. Designed like the Simpsons' living room, it includes a TV that lights up when the alarm sounds. A back-lit LCD clock is embedded into a wall. Requires three C batteries and two AA batteries (not included).

Bart Simpson pajama bag, 1990, Dan Dee. Often mistaken for a doll, this is actually a storage bag with a zipper on the back.

Curtains, 1990. Dreamstyle. 82-by-63-inch "Coordinating Rod Pocket Panels." Design shows Simpsons in various poses. Boxed. . . . .$5-$15.

Night light, Bart, 1990. Street Kids. 4-inch-long Bart-shaped light with electric plug in back. Variations include red, orange and blue shirts. Carded. . . . .$2-$5.

Pajama bag, Bart, 1990. Dan Dee. 24-inch cloth Bart in striped pajamas that unzips in the back to store pajamas. Holds small white pillow in right hand, a mock toothbrush in the other. Carded. . . . . .$30-$45.

Sheet set, twin, 1990. Dreamstyle. One flat sheet, one fitted sheet and one pillow case. Twin set fits 39-by-75-inch mattress. Design shows family members in various poses. Sealed. . . . .$5-$20.

Sheet set, full, 1990. Dreamstyle. One flat sheet, one fitted sheet and two pillow cases. Full set fits 54-by-75-inch mattress. Design shows family members in various poses. Sealed. . . . .$7-$25.

Slumber bag, Bart, "Sleeping's for wimps, man!" 1990. 30-by-57-inch quilted polyester and cotton. For indoor use. Blue-and-white design shows Bart in red pajamas. Sealed. . . . .$30.

Bathroom

Bandages, plastic adhesive, 1990. Quantasia. Twenty-five 3/8-by-3-inch bandage strips. Boxed. . . . .$2-$7.

Bath and shower gel, Bart, 1997. Euromark. U.K. 200-ml bottle. 10 inches high shaped like Bart on a skateboard and wearing a red backpack. Tagged. . . . .$20-$25.

Bath and shower gel, Bart, Maggie and Lisa, 1997. Euromark. U.K. 300-ml bottle. Top shows 5-inch-wide tub with Bart, Lisa and Maggie. Sealed. . . . .$20-$25.

Simpsons plastic adhesive bandages, 1990, Quantasia. Twenty-five ⅜-by-3-inch strips.

Bart Simpson bath and shower gel, 1997, Euromark. U.K. 200-ml bottle.

Bath and shower gel with suction-cup figure, Homer, 1996. Euromark. U.K. 500-ml bottle. Inside is 2-inch figure of Homer. Sealed. . . .$5-$15.

Bath and shower gel with suction-cup figure, Lisa, 1996. Euromark. U.K. 500-ml bottle. Inside is 2-inch figure of Lisa. Sealed. . . . . .5-$15.

Bath and shower gel, Homer and Marge, 1997. Euromark. U.K. 300-ml bottle. Top features 4-inch-wide tub with Homer and Marge. Sealed. . . . .$20-$25.

Bubble bath, Bart, 1990. Cosrich. 8-oz. bottle. Bart's head on top. Sealed. . . . .$5-$8.

Bubble bath, Homer, 1990. Cosrich. 8-oz. bottle. Homer's head on top. Sealed. . . . .$3-$10.

Bubble bath, Lisa, 1990. Cosrich. 8-oz. bottle. Lisa's head on top. Sealed. . . . .$3-$10.

Bubble bath, Marge, 1990. Cosrich. 8-oz. bottle. Marge's head on top. Sealed. . . . .$3-$10.

Foam makeup, 1989. Norben Products. Canada. Tiny metal can with foam makeup. Carded. . . . .$2-$15.

Shampoo, Bart, 1991. Cosrich. 8-oz. bottle. Bart's head of suds on top. Sealed. . . . . . .$5-$8.

Shampoo, Homer, 1991. Cosrich. 8-oz. bottle. Homer's head of suds on top. Sealed. . . . .$5-$8.

Shampoo, Lisa, 1991. Cosrich. 8-oz. bottle. Lisa's head of suds on top. Sealed. . . . .$5-$8.

Shampoo, Maggie, 1991. Cosrich, 8-oz. bottle. Maggie's head of suds on top. Sealed. . . . .$5-$8.

Shampoo, Marge, 1991. Cosrich, 8-oz. bottle. Marge's head of suds on top. Sealed. . . . .$5-$8.

Soap, Bart sculpted, 1990. Cosrich. 3.3-oz. bar of yellow soap sculpted into 5-inch figure. Boxed. . . . .$1-$7.

Soap, finger paint gel, 1990. Cosrich. 4-oz. tube. Variations

Simpsons bubble bath, 1990, Cosrich. 8-oz bottle. Homer, Marge and Bart tops.

include neon green and hot purple. Boxed. . . . .$3-$7.

Soap dish and bath plug, 1996. Euromark. U.K. 4-inch-wide dish with figures of Homer, Marge and Bart. Dish attaches to wall with suction cups. Inside is a small bath plug, with a figure of Bart on top surf-boarding. Sealed. . . . .$10-$15.

Styling gel, radical hair stuff, Bart, 1990. Cosrich. 4-oz. tube. Boxed. . . . .$1-$5.

Sunscreen cream with moisturizer, Bart, 1997. Rebelstorm. Australia. 110-ml tube. Sealed. . . . .$3-$12.

Toothbrush 2-pak, Bart/Lisa, 1991. Harrison. Canada. Boxed. . . . .$1-$7.

Toothbrush 2-pak, Homer/Marge, 1991. Harrison. Canada. Boxed. . . . .$1-$7.

Toothbrush, battery-operated with timer stand, 1990. Helm Products. Includes 2 brushes, battery-operated toothbrush holder, timer stand, and tooth-paste caddy. Battery-operated. . . . .$10-$30.

Toothbrush holder, Bart, 1996. Euromark. U.K. 4-inch plastic with suction cup on back to attach it to the wall. Figure of Bart hangs from front. Includes children's toothbrush. Carded. . .$5-$15.

Towel, beach, Bart with skateboard, "Cool your jets, man!" Juro. 30-by-60-inch red terry cloth. . . . .$15.

Towel, beach, Bart scuba, 1990. Cecil Saydah. 30-by-60-inch white terry cloth. Tagged. . . . .$10-15.

Towel, beach, Bart "Radical Dude!" A La Carte. 30-by-50-inch blue beach towel. . . . .$15.

Towel, beach, Simpsons profiles, 1990. Cecil Saydah. 30-by-60-inch white terry cloth. Design shows heads of Simpsons. Tagged. . . . . .$10-15.

Towel, bath and washcloth, family, 1990. Cecil Saydah. Two-piece set. Bath towel is 24-by-44-inch with white terry cloth showing family posing. Washcloth is 12-by-12-inch with white terry cloth showing Bart. Tagged. . . . .$15-$25.

Bart Simpson sunscreen cream with moisturizer, 1997, Rebelstorm. Australia.

Bart Simpson sculpted soap, 1990, Cosrich. Packaging reads: "Wash it, dude!" and "Now soap has a name and it's Bartholomew J. Simpson, man!"

Bart Simpson "radical" hair-styling gel, 1990, Cosrich. "Spike, scrunch, sculpt and shape."

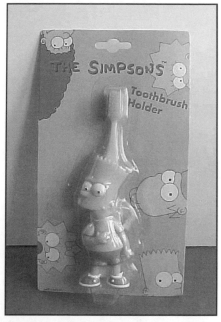

Bart Simpson toothbrush holder, 1996, Euromark. U.K. 4-inch plastic holder with a suction cup on back to attach it to the wall.

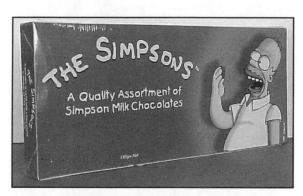

Simpsons milk chocolates, 1997, Confection Concepts. New Zealand. 180-gram gift box with 14 pieces, each shaped like a Simpson.

Simpsons bath and shower gel with Homer and Lisa suction-cup figures, 1996, Euromark. U.K. 500 ml bottles with suction-cup figures inside.

Bart Simpson bubble
bath, 1991,
Grosvenor. U.K. 325-
ml bottle. 9-inch-high
bottle. Originally sold
with paper tag.

Homer Simpson "Atomic Dad" mug with
box, 1990, Presents. 4-inch-high white
mug that shows Homer glowing. Inside
the lip of the cup is Homer's head with
electrons around it.

Bart with scuba gear beach towel, 1990, Cecil
Saydah. 30-by-60-inch white terry cloth.

Homer Simpson "Batch O' Bubbles" bubble bath, 1990, Grosvenor. U.K. 500-ml bottle.

Marge Simpson "World's Best Cook" ceramic mug with box, 1990, Presents. 4-inch-high white mug showing Marge holding steaming food and saying, "Voila!" Inside the lip of the cup is Marge saying, "How 'bout a refill?"

Simpsons bath and shower gel, 1997, Euromark. U.K. 300-ml bottle of bath and shower gel with Bart, Lisa and Maggie on top in 5-inch-wide tub.

Homer Simpson on two-liter bottle of Mug Root Beer, 1997. Simpsons characters appeared on Mug Root Beer, Lipton Brisk Natural Lemon Flavor Iced Tea, Mandarin Orange Slice, Lemon Lime Slice and Josta to promote Fox's giveaway of a full-size replica of the Simpsons house in Nevada. A Kentucky woman won the prize.

Simpsons water bottle, 1997, Headstart. Australia. 6 inches high, with a pop-up lid.

Simpsons "Nuclear Family" ceramic mug with box, 1990, Presents. 4-inch-high white mug showing Simpsons heads as electrons spinning. Inside the lip of the cup is a fallout shelter sign.

Bart Simpson gumball machine, 1990, Jolly Good Industries. 6½ inches high with coin slot in back. Originally sold in green box.

Bart with skateboard beach towel, Juro. 30-by-60 red terry cloth.

Left, Maggie Simpson "Baby Face" ceramic mug, 1990, Presents. 4-inch-high white mug showing Maggie sucking on a pacifier. Inside the lip of the cup is a pacifier image. Lisa Simpson "Overachiever" ceramic mug, 1990, Presents. 4-inch-high white mug. Inside the lip of the mug is Lisa saying, "Phew!"

Bart Simpson finger-paint soap gel, 1990, Crosrich. 4-oz. tube. Neon green and hot purple. Packaging reads: "Paint all kinds of designs in the bathtub without having to tell Mom to cool her jets. She won't get angry because she knows it's the fun way to get clean while you play."

Battery-operated Bart Simpson toothbrush with timer stand, 1990, Helm Products. Push down the big toothbrush to start the timer.

Bart Simpson "Peace Man" ceramic mug with box, 1990, Presents. 4-inch-high white mug showing Bart making peace sign. Inside the lip of the cup is the peace symbol.

Bart "Radical Dude!" beach towel, A La Carte. 30-by-50-inch blue terry cloth.

Bart Simpson foam makeup, 1989, Norben Products. Canada. Metal can. Back of packaging includes instructions for "100 percent skin coverage."

"Cartooning with the Simpsons" book, 1993, Harper Collins. 32 pages. Tips from the folks behind "The Simpsons" on how to draw cartoons like a pro.

Nonfiction books:

"Cartooning with the Simpsons," 1993. Harper Collins. Learn how to draw Simpsons characters. ......$10.

"Fun in the Sun Book," 1992. Harper Collins. Outdoor activities, punctuated with lots of Simpsons humor. ....$11.

Maggie Simpson's "Counting Book," 1991. Harper Collins. Maggie helps young children learn to count. ....$5.

Maggie Simpson's "Book of Animals," 1991. Harper Collins. Maggie helps young children learn about animals. . ...$5.

Maggie Simpson's "Book of Colors and Shapes," 1991. Harper Collins. Maggie helps young children learn about colors and shapes. ....$5.

Maggie Simpson's "Alphabet Book," 1991. Harper Collins. Maggie helps young children learn the alphabet. ....$5.

"Making Faces: A Book of Masks," 1992. HarperPerennial. Cardboard cutout masks of Bart, Lisa, Maggie, Homer, Marge, Milhouse, Otto, Mrs. Krabappel, Grandpa, Moe, Mr. Burns, Apu, Krusty, Itchy and Scratchy. ....$12.

"The Rainy Day Fun Book," 1991. Harper Collins. Indoor activities, punctuated with lots of "inside" jokes. ....$11.

Sheet music, Simpsons theme for piano, 1990. Warner Bros. Publications. Five-page arrangement by Dan Coates of the Simpsons theme music for piano. . ..$5. (Warner also pro-

Simpsons "Sticker Activity Album," 1990, Diamond Publishing. 24 pages. Packets of stickers bound with the album and also sold separately.

duced Simpsons theme sheet music for marching and concert bands, priced at about $40.)

"Simpson Fever," 1990. St. Martin's Paperbacks. 115-page paperback by Jeff Rovin. Unofficial fact and quiz book. . ...$10.

"Simpson Mania," 1990. Consumer Guide. By Steve Dale and Shane Tritsch. 48-page unofficial guide to "The Simpsons," focusing on the first season. Hard cover: $8, glue bound: $7, spiral bound: $6.

"The Simpsons: A Complete Guide to Our Favorite Family," 1997. HarperPerennial. An official episode guide to the first eight seasons. .Hard cover: $25, soft cover: $16.

Sticker Activity Album, Simpsons family, 1990. Diamond Publishing. 24 pages. Includes "Slide-O-Scope" viewer that makes drawings inside appear to move. .$6 without sticker packs, $7 with bag of five sticker packets.

"The Ultra Jumbo Rain-or-Shine Fun Book," 1993. Harper Collins. Combines "The Rainy Day Fun Book" and the "Fun in the Sun Book." . .$14.

"The Unauthorized Guide To The Simpsons Collectibles: A Handbook and Price Guide," 1998. Schiffer Books. Robert W. Getz's 160-page soft-cover guide to Simpsons merchandise. Features more than 500 photos. ......$30.

Books for laughs

"Bart Simpson's Guide to Life: A Wee Handbook for the Perplexed," 1993. Harper Collins. Bart-inspired wisdom. ....$11.

"Bart Simpson's Guide to Life" book, 1993, Harper Collins. 186 pages. Bart's "flavorized morsels of wit, wisdom and worldly knowledge."

"The Rainy Day Fun Book," 1991, Harper Collins. 64 pages. Simpsons puzzles, codes, games, tricks and other indoor activities.

"Bart Simpson's Radical World," 1990. Consumer's Guide. 24-page unofficial soft-cover guide to "The Simpsons." Content aimed at pre-teens. . . . .$10.

"Greeting from The Simpsons: A Postcard Book by Matt Groening," 1990. Harper Collins. A set of post cards. . . . .$10.

"Greeting from The Simpsons: A Postcard Book by Matt Groening," 1990, Harper Collins. 32 full-color Simpsons post cards.

"The Simpsons Xmas Book," 1990, Harper Collins. Hard-cover adaptation of the "The Simpsons Christmas Special" first broadcast Dec. 17, 1989.

Simpsons comic books, including Bartman, Itchy & Scratchy, Krusty the Clown, Lisa and Radioactive Man, 1993-1995, Bongo Entertainment.

"Official Game Secrets: Virtual Bart," for Nintendo and Genesis, 1995. Prima Publishing. Soft-cover guide to Acclaim computer game. . . . .$13.

"The Simpsons Guide to Springfield," 1998. HarperPerennial. 128-page, soft-cover spoof of tourist guide books. . . . .$14.

"The Simpsons Poster Book," 1990. Button-Up. Eight tear-out posters, featuring Homer and Bart, Marge and Maggie, Bart with slingshot, Bartman, Lisa, Maggie, the family dancing, and Bart on skateboard. . . . .$10.

"The Simpsons Uncensored Family Album," 1991. Harper Collins. Mock soft-cover scrap book tracing the lives of the Simpsons. $10.

"The Simpsons Xmas Book," 1990. Harper Collins. Adaptation of the "The Simpsons Christmas Special." Hard cover: $10, soft cover: $12.

Bongo comic books

"Bart Simpson's Joke Book," June 1995. Mini-

"Official Game Secrets: Virtual Bart" book for Nintendo and Genesis, 1995, Prima Publishing. Soft-cover guide to the Acclaim computer game.

size promotional issue from Bongo published in Hero Illustrated magazine. Sealed. . . . . . .$7-$15.

"Bartman and Radioactive Man," 1994. Mini-size promotional issue from Bongo published in Hero Illustrated magazine. . . . .$7.

"Simpsons Comics and Stories," 1993. First Simpsons comic book. An issue of Simpsons Illustrated magazine. Includes Bartman poster. Sealed. . . . .$5-$10.

"Bartman" No. 1, 1993. Extra-thick cover printed in silver-colored ink. Includes Bartman poster. . .$7.

"Bartman" Nos. 2-6, 1994-95. Issue 3 contains Skybox promo "spinner card" with Radioactive Man. No. 3 is $5, others $4 each.

"Itchy & Scratchy" Holiday Hi-Jinx Special No. 1, 1994. . . . .$7.

"Itchy & Scratchy" No. 1, 1993. Includes Itchy & Scratchy poster. .$7.

"Itchy & Scratchy" Nos. 2-3, 1994. No. 3 contains part one of "When Bongos Collide Crossover!" as well as decoder card for Simpsons Skybox trading cards Series II. . . . .$5 each.

"Krusty" No. 1, 1995. First of three parts, "The Rise and Fall of Krustyland." . . . .$7.

"Krusty" Nos. 2-3, 1995. Final two parts of "The Rise and Fall of Krustyland." . . . .$5 each.

"Lisa" No. 1, 1995. Sole comic in Lisa line. .$5.

"Radioactive Man" No. 1, 1993. Includes Radioactive Man poster. Dated "November 1952." . . . .$7.

"Radioactive Man" 80-page special, 1995. .$7.

"Radioactive Man" No. 88, 1994. Dated "May 1962." . . . .$5.

"Radioactive Man" No. 216, 1994. Dated "August 1972." . . . .$5.

"Radioactive Man" No. 412, 1994. Includes Radioactive Man Skybox Series II promo card B2.

Dated "October 1980." . . . .$5.

"Radioactive Man" No. 679, 1994. Includes Radioactive Man Skybox Series II promo card B6. Dated "January 1986." . . . .$5.

"Radioactive Man" No. 1000, 1994. Dated "January 1995." . . .
. . . .$5.

"Simpsons" No. 1, 1993. Includes Simpsons poster.
. . . .$10.

"Simpsons" Nos. 2-5, 1993. No. 4 includes Willy "The Dupe" Dipkin baseball player on a Skybox Series II promo card B1. No. 5 includes Black Belch Skybox Series II Smell-O-Rama promo card B4. .$5 for No. 4 or No. 5, $4 for each of the others.

"Simpsons" Nos. 6-44, 1994-99. . . . .$3 each.

"Treehouse of Horror" No. 1, October 1995.
. . . .$7.

"Treehouse of Horror" No. 2, October 1996. "Spooktacular Second Issue." . . . .$5.

"Treehouse of Horror" No. 3, October 1997. "Third Throat-Throttling Issue." . .$5.

"Treehouse of Horror" No. 4, October 1998. "Fourth Fright-Filled Issue." . . . .$5.

Bongo reprints

"Simpsons Comics Big Bonanza," 1998. HarperPerennial. Soft-cover reprint of Simpsons Comics 28-31. . . . .$12.

"Simpsons Comics Extravaganza," 1994. HarperPerennial. Soft-cover reprint of Simpsons Comics 1-4. . . . .$12.

"Simpsons Comics on Parade" book, 1996 & 1998. Harper Perennial. 120 pages. Soft-cover reprint of Simpsons Comics 24-27

"Simpsons Comics Big Bonanza" book, 1998. Harper Perennial. 117 pages. Soft-cover reprint of Simpsons Comics 28-31

Simpsons Illustrated magazines, 1991-1993, Welsh Publishing Group. Now-defunct official publication.

"Simpsons Comics Spectacular," 1994 and 1995. HarperPerennial. Soft-cover reprint of Simpsons Comics 6-9, ...$12.

"Bartman: Best of the Best," 1994 and 1995. HarperPerennial. Soft-cover reprint of Bartman comics 1-3, Itchy & Scratchy 3, and Simpsons Comics 5. . . . .$12

"Simpsons Comics on Parade," 1996 and 1998. HarperPerennial. Soft-cover reprint of Simpsons Comics 24-27. . . . .$12.

"Simpsons Comics Simpsorama," 1995 and 1996. Bongo Comics Group. Soft-cover reprint of Simpsons Comics 11-14. . . . .$12.

"Simpsons Comics Strike Back!" 1996. Bongo Comics Group. Soft-cover reprint of Simpsons Comics 15-18. . . . .$10.

"Simpsons Comics Wing Ding," 1996 and 1997. Bongo Comics Group. Soft-cover reprint of Simpsons Comics 19-23. . . . .$12.

Magazines

Simpsons Illustrated

Spring 1991, Volume 1, Number 1. 42 pages. This now-defunct official Simpsons magazine printed cartoons, behind-the-scenes stories about the show, original humor, letters from fans, and lots more. The cover: Bart, chalk in hand, stands in front of a blackboard where he's written multiple times: "I will not read this magazine in class." . . . .$10.

Summer 1991, Volume 1, Number 2. 40 pages. The cover: Homer is startled by an alarm at his

Book reviews

"The Simpsons Guide to Springfield"

($13.95, Harper Perennial, 1998) is a hilarious spoof of tourist guide books. (It's even billed as being part of an "Are We There Yet?" series.) This book is packed with colorful artwork, Simpsons humor, and inevitable insights into small-city life in America. Probably in Canada, too.

Created by the folks from Bongo who produce the Simpsons comics, this 128-page soft-cover book is probably best consumed at more than one sitting. Like the show itself, there is so much here that it takes a while to absorb it all.

After an essay offering a "historical perspective" on Springfield, there are chapters devoted to the city's attractions, lodging, dining, shopping and annual events. Having more than 200 television episodes from which to pluck ideas definitely hasn't hurt this book. In the chapter on attractions, there are references to Itchy & Scratchy Land, Springfield Gorge, Barney's Bowlarama, and even the bullet that shot Mr. Burns. (We won't spoil the joke by telling you where you can find it in Springfield.)

"The Unauthorized Guide To The Simpsons Collectibles: A Handbook and Price Guide"

($29.95, Schiffer Books, 1998) is a 160-page soft-cover book by longtime Simpsons collector Robert W. Getz.

The 8-1/2-by-11-inch glossy pages are packed with more than 500 color photos and brief descriptions of the best-known Simpsons dolls, action figures, trading cards, key rings, buttons, record albums and other retail merchandise. There are also harder-to-find items listed here, including books, card games and other merchandise produced for markets outside the U.S.

The author lists with each

nuclear-plant work station, where he's been drinking coffee and eating a doughnut. . . . . $10.

Fall 1991, Volume 1, Number 3. 36 pages. The cover: Lisa plays saxophone while Bart yells, "Lemme outta here, man!" . . . .$10.

Winter 1992, Volume 1, Number 4. 38 pages. The cover: Krusty the Clown is shown reading Simpsons Illustrated and saying, "Give a hoot! Buy this magazine!" . . . .$10.

Spring 1992, Volume 1, Number 5. 36 pages. The cover: scene of underwater-diving Bart and Homer approaching an octopus that looks stunningly like Homer. Bart says, "Whoa! That's one ugly octopus, man!" . . . .$12.

Summer 1992, Volume 1, Number 6. 46 pages. The cover: skateboarding Bart does a dangerous flip outside the kitchen window, startling Marge inside. . . . .$12.

Fall 1992, Volume 1, Number 7. 40 pages. The cover: Nancy Cartwright, the voice of Bart, holds her hand over the mouth of this cartoon bad boy. Headline reads, "The Voice of Bart Speaks! An Exclusive Interview with NANCY CARTWRIGHT." . . . .$12.

Annual 1992. (No volume number.) 32 pages. Bound into the magazine are two pairs of 3-D glasses. The cover: Homer, Marge, Lisa, Bart and Maggie wear 3-D glasses. Headline reads, "1992 annual in mind-bending, knee-slapping, eye-popping 3-D." . . . .$12.

Winter 1993, Volume 1, Number 8. 42 pages. The cover: Bart, arms folded, displays a skull and crossbones tattoo that reads, "Eat my shorts." Headline reads, "Rude, Crude and Tattooed, Dude!" . . . .$15.

Simpsons Comics and Stories, Issue No. 1. 1993. 34 pages. First Simpsons comic book. The cover: Headlined, "A special publication of Simpsons Illustrated," this comic-book size publication shows Bartman on the cover, arms folded, saying, "Watch it, man!" It was originally sold sealed in a

Animation magazine, Fall 1989. Cover story: "The Simpsons: Prime Time Animation."

Cracked magazine, December 1994. Cover shows O.J. Simpson with a Bart-shaped head saying, "I didn't do it, man."

plastic bag with 26-by-20-inch poster of Radioactive Man and Bartman posing. . . . .$8.

Summer 1993, Volume 1, Number 9. 40 pages. The cover: A stunned-looking Simpsons creator Matt Groening is surrounded by cartoon faces of Marge, Bart, Maggie, Lisa and Homer. Headline reads, "Meet Matt! An exclusive interview with Matt Groening, the man behind the Simpsons!" . . . .$15.

Other U.S.

Animation, Fall 1989. "The Simpsons: Prime Time Animation." . . . .$5.

Animation, January 1996. "10 Year Anniversary." . . . .$3.

Animation, October 1995. "The Simpsons Enter the Fourth Dimension." . . . .$10.

Cards Illustrated magazine, September 1994. "Simpsons. Creator Matt Groening on Homer, Marge and Trading Cards!" . . . .$5.

Comics Scene Spectacular magazine, July 1990. With Simpsons poster. . . . .$5.

Cracked, April 1996. No. 106. "Best of TV." Cover shows Bart and other TV characters crashing into the surf. . . . .$3.

Cracked, December 1994. "America's #1 TV Show" Cover shows O.J. Simpson with a Bart-shaped head saying, "I didn't do it, man." . . . .$3.

Cracked, November 1990. "Exclusive Simpsons Interview." Cover shows an angry Bart with a slingshot taking aim at a Ninja Turtle. . . . .$3.

Cracked, October 1990. "Bart Simpson: #1 Brat." Cover shows

Cards Illustrated magazine, September 1994. Cover story: "Simpsons Creator Matt Groening on Homer, Marge and Trading Cards!"

Disney Adventures magazine, February 1994. Cover story: "Bart Rocks! Bartman Comic Inside."

Hot Dog magazine, No. 65, 1991, Scholastic. Cover story: "TV's Favorite Families!"

Previews magazine, Volume 3, No. 10, October 1993. Cover story: "Bart Goes Bongo!"

wanted posters of Bart, New Kids and others. .$3.

Cracked, October 1993. "Year of the Brat." Cover shows Dennis the Menace, Bart Simpson and other troublemakers. . . . .$3.

Cracked, September 1990. "Exclusive Comics Movie and TV Club." Cover shows Bart and other characters. . . . .$3.

Disney Adventures, February 1994. "Bart Rocks! Bartman Comic Inside." Cover shows Bart and Lisa. . . . .$5.

Entertainment Weekly, May 8, 1990. "The Making of 'The Simpsons' - The Art of Bart." In-depth look at how an episode is made. Includes feature on merchandise. . . . .$15.

Entertainment Weekly, Aug. 31, 1990. "Can Bill Beat Bart?" Cover shows comedian Bill Cosby wearing a Bart T-shirt. . . . .$5.

Flux, Issue No. 6, 1995. "Simpsons Invasion: An Inside Look at Bart's Sick & Twisted New Comic." . . . .$10.

Hot Dog, No. 65, 1991. Scholastic. "TV's Favorite Families!" Cover shows Simpsons. . . . .$5.

Keyboard, January 1993. "The Anatomy of Scoring a TV Show: The Simpsons." Cover story on composing music for the series. . . . .$8.

Mad, No. 299. December 1990. "In This Issue We Mow Down ... The Simpsons & Total Recall." Cover shows head shot of Bart. $3.

Previews, Volume 3, No. 10. October 1993. "Bart Goes Bongo!" Cover shows Bartman and Radioactive Man. Includes sheet with reproductions of four promo cards for Skybox's Series I trading cards. . . . .$10.

Rolling Stone, June 28, 1990. "At Home with Bart Simpson. Underachiever or Just a Kid?" . . . .$10.

TV Guide, March 17-23, 1990. "TV: The good, the bad and the ugly. By The Simpsons, TV's hot new primetime family." . . . .$10.

TV Guide, Nov. 28, 1992. "Maggie Speaks! We ask famous fans what she'll say." . . . .$5.

TV Guide, Oct. 21, 1995. Includes three-page "mini-comic" celebrating the annual Halloween episode of "The Simpsons." . . . . . .$10.

TV Guide, Jan. 3, 1998. Four different Simpsons covers that, when placed side by side, form a couch scene. . . . .$4 each.

Wizard, No. 28, December 1993. Cover shows Bartman with Radioactive Man. . . . .$3.

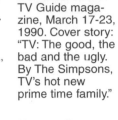

TV Guide magazine, March 17-23, 1990. Cover story: "TV: The good, the bad and the ugly. By The Simpsons, TV's hot new prime time family."

Entertainment Weekly magazine, Aug. 31, 1990. Cover story: "Can Bill Beat Bart?" Comedian Bill Cosby wears a Bart shirt.

Non-U.S.

Loaded, August 1996. U.K. "Look Bart We're Famous." . . . .$5.

Radio Times, November 1996. U.K. "BBC TV interrupts its normal service to bring you THE SIMPSONS." . . .$5.

TV Guide, Dec. 26, 1998-Jan. 1, 1999. Canada. Cover features Homer and Marge. Cover story on "The Art of Making Bart." . . . .$5.

Radio Times magazine, November 1996. U.K. Cover story: "BBC TV interrupts its normal service to bring you THE SIMPSONS."

Mad magazine, No. 299. December 1990. Cover story: "In This Issue We Mow Down ... The Simpsons & Total Recall."

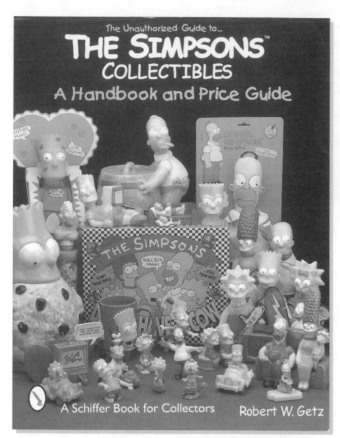

"The Unauthorized Guide To The Simpsons Collectibles: A Handbook and Price Guide" book, 1998, Schiffer Books. By Robert W. Getz. Review on Page 114.

"Simpson Mania" book, 1990, Consumer Guide. By Steve Dale and Shane Tritsch. 48-page unofficial guide to the first season of "The Simpsons" and early merchandise. Review on Page 29.

"The Simpsons Guide to Springfield" book, 1998, HarperPerennial. 128-page soft-cover spoof of tourist guide books. Review on Page 114.

17 Clothing and accessories

T-shirts

Bart, "Cool your jets, man," 1990. SSI. White shirt shows Bart leaning on a skateboard and saying, "Cool your jets, man!" "Bart Simpson" is printed on the bottom. . . . .$10.

Bart, "Future All-Star," 1990. Baby-size shirt showing Bart spinning a basketball and the caption "Future All-Star.. . . . .$5.

Bart, "Gimme a break!" 1990. SSI. Blue shirt showing Bart, arms folded, saying "Gimme a break!" Below him is the caption "Bart Simpson.. . . . .$5.

Bart, "I didn't do it …," 1990. Argo. White shirt showing a grinning Bart, tip-toeing, saying, "I didn't do it. Nobody saw me do it. You can't prove anything.. . . . .$5.

Bart, photographing butt, 1997. Stanley DeSantis. Design shows a smiling Bart, his shorts pulled down to expose his butt, taking a picture of it in a mirror. Underneath is the caption "Bartholomew J. Simpson.. . . . .$15.

Bart, Maxell parody, 1996. Stanley DeSantis. Design is parody of Maxell commercial where a man is blown back watching TV. . . . . $15.

Bart, Rene Magritte apple painting parody, 1995. Stanley DeSantis. Design shows apple in front of yellow face of Bart, with just the top of his head showing. . . . .$15.

Bart, skull and crossbones, 1997. Littlefield, Adams & Co. Black T-shirt

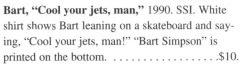

Bart Simpson "Future All-Star" T-shirt, 1990. Infant-size.

Bart Simpson skull and crossbones T-shirt, 1997, Littlefield, Adams & Co. Gold-colored design showing Bart's head as a skull and crossbones.

Bart Simpson photographing butt T-shirt, 1997, Stanley DeSantis. Bart expose his button for a snap shot.

with gold-colored design showing Bart's head as a skull and crossbones. . . .$10.

Bart "Underachiever — and proud of it, man!" 1989. Changes. Design features Bart with slingshot. Top says "Bart Simpson: Underachiever," and Bart adds, "And proud of it, man!". . .$20.

Bartman, on skateboard, 1990. Screen Stars Best. Design shows Bartman on skateboard. Underneath is caption "Bartman".. . . . .$10.

Family, "Family Bonding," 1989. Royal First Class. White shirt shows family sitting on couch, watching TV. Everyone looks happy, except Bart, who has a scowl. . . .$10.

Homer, "All-American Dad," 1990. SSI Express. White shirt shows Homer, arms outstretched, saying "Why you little —!. . . .$10.

Bart Simpson Maxell parody T-shirt, 1996, Stanley DeSantis. Parody of Maxell commercial. Bart holds a remote control as he watches Krusty the Clown on TV.

Bart Simpson "The Great War" parody T-shirt, 1995, Stanley DeSantis. Bart, apple in front of his face, in parody of in Rene Magritte painting.

117

Homer Simpson "Got Beer?" T-shirt, 1995, Stanley DeSantis. Caption reads, "Got beer?" as Homer munches on a pretzel, mouth puckered from the salt.

Homer, "Couch Potato," 1995, Logotel. White and gray shirt featuring Homer in underwear with remote control. . . . .$15.

Homer, "Doesn't Wear Khakis," 1995. Stanley DeSantis. Design shows Homer sitting on couch in his underwear. . . . .$15.

Homer, "Got Beer?" 1995. Stanley DeSantis. Design shows Homer munching on a pretzel, mouth puckered from the salt, and the caption "Got beer?. . . . .$15.

Homer, hologram, 1996. Stanley DeSantis. White shirt has 3-by-2½-inch hologram stitched on front of the shirt. Hologram shows Homer tossing a donut into his mouth. . . . .$15.

Homer, "Intel Inside," 1998. Intel. Design over left breast pocket showing back of Homer's head with an "Intel Inside" stamped on it. . . . .$15.

Homer, "Homersapien," 1996. Stanley DeSantis. Design is parody of the evolution of man drawings. This one begins with a monkey eating a banana (Monkius Eatalotis) and evolves over five drawings into Homer, clad only in undershorts and holding a banana (Homersapien). . . . .$15.

Homer, "Just Donut," 1996, Stanley DeSantis. Design shows Homer in T-shirt, shorts and sneakers, athletically leaping after a donut. . . . .$15.

Homer, "Modern Man," 1995. Logotel. Design shows cross-section of Homer's brain, divided into such sections as "Today's winning lottery number," "Beer," "Naptime," "Where are my socks?" "Last night's episode of Baywatch," and "Dirty limericks." . . . .$15.

Homer, "Woo Hoo!" 1997. Stanley DeSantis. Design shows Homer with fist raised in an expression of happiness. . . . .$15.

Lisa, "The Screech," 1995. Stanley DeSantis. Design features Lisa, hands

Homer Simpson "Intel Inside" T-shirt, 1998, Intel. 1998 promotional item from Intel, manufacturer of computer processors.

Lisa Simpson "The Screech" parody T-shirt, 1995, Stanley DeSantis. Lisa, hands to face screaming, in a parody of the Edvard Munch painting.

to face screaming, in a parody of the Edvard Munch painting. . . $15. . . . .

Mr. Burns, "Who Shot Mr. Burns?" 1995. Stanley DeSantis. Design features Mr. Burns clutching his chest. Around him are mug shots of various characters who became suspects in his shooting. . . . .$20.

"The Simpsons Sing the Blues," 1990. Stedman. White shirt shows various Simpsons characters singing or playing musical instruments. Shirt part of a mail-in offer to buyers of Geffen Records' "The Simpsons Sing the Blues" compact disc or cassette. (Offer has expired.) . . . .$20.

Miscellaneous clothing

Baseball-style cap, Bart. American Needle. Purple cap with stitching of Bart's face on front. Tagged. . . . .$7-$12.

Baseball-style cap, Bart "Alone," 1996. The Planet. Black cap with sleepy-looking Bart. . .$10.

Baseball-style cap, Bart "Radical Dude," 1990. Universal. Pink nylon-type fabric cap with Bart on front. . . . .$5.

Baseball-style cap, Homer, "Intel Inside," 1998. Intel. Black cap with back of Homer's head on which is printed the Intel logo. . . . . . .$10.

Baseball-style cap, Homer. American Needle. Homer's smiling face on front, donut on side. Tagged. . . . .$7-$12.

Baseball-style cap, Marge. American Needle. Marge's smiling face on front, hair spray on side. Tagged.$7-$12.

Baseball-style cap, Maggie. American Needle. Maggie

Homer Simpson "Just Donut" T-shirt, 1996, Stanley DeSantis. Caption reads, "Just donut" as Homer athletically leaps to grab a donut.

sucking pacifier on front, pacifier on side. Tagged. . . . .$7-$12.

Shirt, long-sleeved, Bart, "The Many Moods of Bart," 1990. Allison. Gray shirt with blue collar. Design shows four faces of Bart. . . . .$10.

Shirt, long-sleeved, Bart, "Comin' through, man!" 1990. Allison. Black shirt with yellow collar. Design shows Bart on skateboard. . . . . . .$10.

Shorts, holiday boxer, Bart. St. Tropez. Australia. Silk. Design features Bart in Santa hat and the words, "Ho, ho, man!" Tagged. .$10-$25.

Shorts, family waving, 1990. Boxer Rebellion. White shorts with 8-inch high drawing of the Simpsons on upper left thigh area. . . . .$10.

Socks, Bart in cap, "Go for it, man!" 1997. Target Australia. Thick black socks (shoe size 2-8) with head of Bart. . . . .$3-$8.

Socks, Bart with butterfly net, 1993. Sox for Tot. Carded. . . . .$1-$5.

Socks, Bart posing, 1996. Sock Shop. U.K. Children's cotton-nylon socks showing Bart alone. Tagged. . . . . $5-$10.

Sweat pants, Bart, "Sit on it, man!" 1990. Children's blue pants with Bart's head on rump area saying, "Sit on it, man!" One leg of the pants has "Bart Simpson" in big red lettering. . . . . .$10.

Sweatshirt, Bart "Don't have a cow, man!" 1990. SSI. Dark blue shirt with design that shows Bart, arms outstretched, saying, "Don't have a cow, man!." . . . .$15.

Sweatshirt, Bart "Jingle Bells," 1990. SSI. Black shirt with design that shows Bart singing, "Jingle Bells, Batman smells, Robin laid an egg. Batmobile, broke it's (sic) wheel, and Joker got away." Bart sang this in the first Christmas special. . . . .$20.

Sweatshirt, Bartman, 1990. SSI. White shirt with design that shows Bartman on skateboard. . . .$15.

Sweatshirt, Lisa "Queen of the Blues," 1990. Blue shirt shows Lisa playing saxophone with music notes coming from the instrument. . . . .$10.

Tank top, Bart, "No way, man," 1990. Gesim

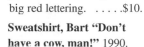
Bart Simpson "Go for it, man!" children's socks, 1997, Target Australia.

Bart Simpson children's socks, 1996, Sock Shop. U.K. Cotton-nylon on display card.

Corp. France. Black sleeveless shirt showing Bart, grimacing with arms folded, saying, "No way, man!. . . . .$5.

Neck ties

Bart, head shot, 1993. Balancine. Silk. Blue starry sky with the top of Bart's head sticking up from the bottom. . . . .$30.

Bart, "I will not waste chalk," 1996. Balancine. Silk. Bart in front of a blackboard filled with the phrase, "I will not waste chalk.. . . . .$20.

Bart and Homer surfing, 1994. Balancine. Silk. Bart surfs a wave about to crash into a screaming Homer in a leaky inner tube. . . . .$25.

Family, various head shots, 1993. Balancine. Silk. Flowery pattern, along with heads of Marge, Homer, Bart, Lisa and Maggie. . . . .$30.

Homer, "Bowlarama," 1993. Balancine. Silk. Homer bowling. . . . .$30.

Homer, "I'm going to lose my job," 1998. Ralph Marlin. Polyester. A sweating Homer and the caption. "Oh, I'm going to lose my job because I'm dangerously unqualified.. . . . .$15.

Itchy and Scratchy, "Bang," 1993. Balancine. Silk. Weapons-wielding cat and dog injuring each other with large "BANG" lettering throughout. . . . .$30.

Moe's Last Chance Diner. Balancine. Silk. Five rows of bar stools, each with a member of the family sitting on it. . . . .$30.

Simpsons faces, 1994. Balancine. Silk. Black tie with tops of family members' heads peeking in from sides. . . . .$25.

Homer Simpson "I'm going to lose my job" neck tie, 1998, Ralph Marlin. Polyester.

Accessories

Bow Biters, Bart, 1990. Brookside. Clips lock and hold laces in place. Figural Bart on each of 2 biters. Carded. . . . .$2-$7.

Earrings, Bart, 1990. N.J. Croce. Pair are each about 1½ inches long and feature a full-length image of Bart on white plastic. Carded. . . .$4-$8.

Belt, stretch, Bart, "Right on, dude!" 1990.

Pyramid Industries. Black stretch belt with a circular button on front showing a smiling Bart. Carded. . . . .$5-$15.

Belt bag, 1990. Imaginings. Also known as a "fanny pack," this zippered bag features design with heads of Homer and Bart. Variations include purple and blue. Bagged. . . . .$5-10.

Hair clip, Lisa, "What a moron!" 1990. Wow Wee Products. 2¾-inch chip showing Lisa. Carded. . . . .$1-$3.

Hair clip, Bart, "Cowabunga dude!" 1990. Wow Wee Products. Canada. 2¾-inch clip shows Bart on surfboard and the saying, "Cowabunga dude!" Canadian. Carded. . . . .$1-$3.

Hair clip, Bart, "Don't have a cow, man!" 1990. Wow Wee Products. Canada. 2¾-inch clip shows Bart. Carded. . . . .$1-$3.

Hair clip, family, 1990. Wow Wee Products. Canada. 2¾-inch clip shows Homer choking Bart. Carded. . . . .$1-$3.

Head band, Lisa, 1990. Wow Wee Products. Canada. Lisa's face shown along top of band. Carded. . . .$1-$3.

Head band, Bart, 1990, Wow Wee Products. Canada. Bart's face shown along top of band. Carded. . . .$1-$3.

Ponytail holder, Lisa, "Cool hair," 1990. Wow Wee Products. Canada. Elastic band attached to two circular designs. Carded. . . . .$1-$3

Ponytail holder, family, 1990. Wow Wee Products. Canada. Elastic band attached to two circular designs. Carded. . . . .$1-$3.

Ponytail holder, Bart, "Don't have a cow, man!" 1990. Wow Wee Products. Canada. Elastic band attached to two circular designs. Carded. . . . .$1-$3.

Ponytail holder, Bart, "Back off, dude!" 1990. Wow Wee Products. Canada. Elastic band attached to two circular designs. Carded. . . . .$1-$3.

Rain coat, family, 1990. Red vinyl. Children's size with metal buckles and draw string. . . . . .$5.

Shoe laces, 40-inch, 1990. Chadwick Industries. White laces with faces of Bart, Lisa and Maggie. Carded. . . . .$1-$3.

Slippers, Bart, 1990. Made of soft, blue cloth with a doll-like figure of Bart's head popping out of the top. Boxed. . . . .$5-$15.

Slippers, family, 1990. Chadwick Industries.

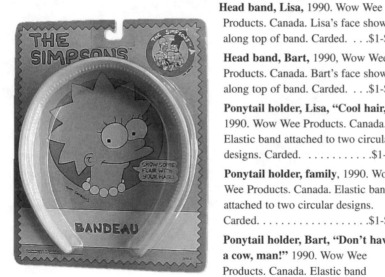

Lisa Simpson head band, 1990, Wow Wee Products. Canada. Top of band displays Lisa's face.

Light blue with furry cloth inside and out. 2-inch plastic decal on side shows Simpsons posing. Boxed. . . . .$10-$20.

Slippers, Homer "Amazing Feets," 1995. Spencer Gifts. Foot-long heavily padded yellow slippers with the face of Homer popping out the front with a dangling tongue. Tagged. . . .$10-$20.

Sneakers, Bart, 1990. Chadwick Industries. Children's footwear that's white with blue and red trim. Top of tongues shows family posing. Boxed. . . . .$5-$20

Stretch suspenders, Bart, 1990. Pyramid Industries. Black suspenders with face of Bart in spot where they cross. Carded. . . . .$5-$15.

Umbrella, Bart with skateboard, 1991. Shaw Creations. Approximately 30-inch diameter clear plastic umbrella with images of Bart. Metal frame and a light-blue plastic handle. Delicate clear-plastic sheath. Tagged. . . . .$20-$30.

Wallet, Bart and Lisa, 1990. Imaginings. 5¼-by-3½ inches. Pink and black vinyl with tiny heads of Bart and Lisa in various poses. Carded. . .$7-$12.

Wallet, Bart "Big spender," 1990, Imaginings. Blue vinyl with dollar signs all over. as well as Bart burning money. Carded. . . . .$7-$12.

Bart Simpson "Big spender" wallet, 1990, Imaginings. Comes with a clear plastic sleeve for your favorite photos.

Wallet, family members, 1996. U.K. Design shows Marge and Homer hugging. Sealed. $3-$12.

Wallet, Lisa, "A penny saved: a pony earned," 1990, Imaginings. Green vinyl with cent signs all over, as well as Lisa holding a purse and dreaming of a horse. Carded. . . . .$7-$10.

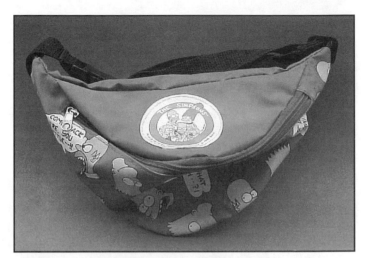

Simpsons belt bag, 1990, Imaginings. Zippered bag can be attached around the waist.

Bart Simpson stretch suspenders, 1990, Pyramid Industries. Card notes: "One size fits all!"

Bart Simpson cap, mid-1990s, American Needle. Purple cap with stitching of Bart's face on front, a slingshot on side, and "BART" on back.

Baby Bart Simpson bib, 1992, Binky.

Bartman sweatshirt, 1990,

Bart Simpson "Back off, dude!"
ponytail holder, 1990, Wow Wee
Products. Canada.

Bart Simpson "Sit on it, man!" sweat pants, 1990. Children's blue sweat pants with Bart's head on bottom. Front leg has "Bart Simpson" in large red lettering.

Bart Simpson Bow Biters, 1990, Brookside. The clips help to keep shoelaces tied. Instructions on back of display card.

Bart Simpson "Jingle Bells" sweat-shirt, 1990, SSI. Bart sings "Jingle Bells, Batman smells, Robin laid an egg. Batmobile, broke it's (sic) wheel, and Joker got away." He sung the tune in the first Simpsons Christmas special.

Homer Simpson "All-American Dad" cap, 1990,
Universal.

Bart Simpson "The Many Moods
of Bart" long-sleeved shirt, 1990,
Allison.

Bart Simpson holiday boxer shorts, St. Tropez.
Australia. Silk design features Bart in Santa hat
and the words, "Ho, ho, man!"

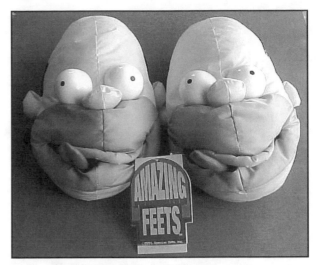

Homer Simpson "Amazing Feets" slippers, 1995, Spencer Gifts. 1-foot-long, shaped like Homer's head.

Homer Simpson "All-American Dad" T-shirt, 1990, SSI Express.

Bart Simpson stretch belt, 1990, Pyramid Industries. Circular button on front shows Bart saying, "Right on, dude!"

Bart Simpson children's socks, 1993, Sox for Tot.

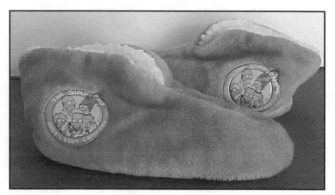

Simpsons slippers, 1990, Chadwick Industries. Light blue with furry cloth inside. On the sides are 2-inch plastic decals showing the Simpsons.

Homer Simpson "Doesn't Wear Khakis" T-shirt, 1995, Stanley DeSantis.

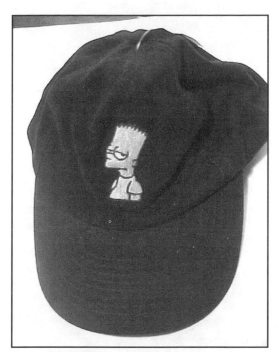

Bart Simpson "Alone" cap, 1996, The Planet.

Lisa Simpson "Queen of the Blues" sweatshirt, 1990.

Bart Simpson slippers, 1990. Soft blue cloth with Bart's head popping out of the tops.

Simpsons Wave 2 home videos box set (volumes 4, 5 and 6), 1997, Fox Video.

Simpsons Wave 3 home videos box set (volumes 7, 8 and 9), 1998, Fox Video.

Simpsons Wave 4 home videos box set (volumes 10, 11 and 12), 1999, Fox Video. The set includes a now-expired mail-in offer for Homer boxer shorts.

Interview: Alf Clausen

Alf Clausen, composer of music for "The Simpsons," discussed in 1997 his choice of music for "Songs in the Key of Springfield," the album from Rhino Records featuring songs and other clips from the show.

Q: Can you think of a couple of different songs on there that you decided definitely to include because they are fan favorites?

Alf: Yes, there is one in particular: Homer's rendition of "It Was a Very Good Year" that he turned into "It Was a Very Good Beer." That was not in the original assemblage that I put together. But it just seemed wherever I went, that title kept popping up, and I thought: Boy, that's too good to pass up.

Q: I heard, too, that "See My Vest" is kind of a cult favorite.

Alf: That's another track that people have suggested we might have a single on.

Q: How late could you include songs? Because I know there aren't any from the recent "Mary Poppins" parody in there.

Alf: Right. And one of the reasons for doing that is I didn't want to include any songs of ("Simpsons") shows that hadn't aired yet.

At the time when all of the final determinations were being made as to what we could include and what we couldn't include (on the album), we didn't have an air date for that show yet. And so I just made the decision that it would be nice to hold off on that. We're all crossing our fingers that this will be very successful and that there will be a Volume Two so we can include some of these things, not only the "Mary Poppins" tracks, but the Maison Derriere song (in episode "Bart After Dark"). I don't know if you saw that one a few weeks back ... where Bart is employed in the local house of ill repute.

Home videos

"The Simpsons Christmas Special," 1991. Fox Video. First Simpsons Christmas special, which originally aired in 1989 as "Simpsons Roasting on an Open Fire." Sealed. . . . .$4-$10.

Volume One, "There's No Disgrace Like Home"/"Life On The Fast Lane," 1997. Fox Video. Includes short "Family Portrait" from "The Tracey Ullman Show." Also sold as part of a three-cassette box set with volumes 2 and 3. Sealed. .$5-$10 for single, $15-$25 for box set.

Volume Two, "Bart The General"/"Moaning Lisa," 1997. Fox Video. Includes short "The Funeral" from "The Tracey Ullman Show." Sealed. .$5-$10.

Volume Three, "The Crepes Of Wrath"/"Krusty Gets Busted," 1997. Fox Video. Includes short "The Aquarium" from "The Tracey Ullman Show." Sealed. $5-$10.

Volume Four, "Treehouse Of Horror (The Simpsons Halloween Special)"/"Bart Gets An F," 1997. Fox Video. Includes short "Bart's Haircut" from "The Tracey Ullman Show." Also sold as part of a three-cassette box set with volumes 5 and 6. Sealed. . . . .$5-$10 for single,$15-$25 for box set.

Volume Five, "Two Cars In Every Garage And Three Eyes On Every Fish"/"Bart vs. Thanksgiving," 1997. Fox Video. Includes short "Scary Movie" from "The Tracey Ullman Show." Sealed. . . . .$5-$10.

Volume Six, "Bart The Daredevil"/"Itchy, Scratchy & Marge," 1997. Fox Video. Includes short "The Bart Simpson Show" from "The Tracey Ullman Show." Sealed. . . . .$5-$10.

Volume Seven, "Bart Gets Hit By A Car"/"One Fish, Two Fish, Blowfish, Blue Fish," 1998. Fox Video. Includes short "Shut Up Simpsons" from

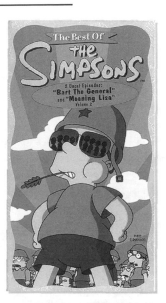

Simpsons home video Volume Two, "Bart The General" and "Moaning Lisa," 1997, Fox Video.

"The Tracey Ullman Show." Also sold as part of a three-cassette box set with volumes 8 and 9. Sealed.$5-$10 for single, . . .$15-$25 for box set.

Volume Eight, "The Way We Was"/"Homer Vs. Lisa and the 8th Commandment," 1998. Fox Video. Includes short "Family Therapy" from "The Tracey Ullman Show." Sealed. . . . .$5-$10.

Volume Nine, "Three Men And A Comic Book"/"Lisa's Substitute," 1998. Fox Video. Includes first two parts of short "Zoo Story" from "The Tracey Ullman Show." Sealed. .$5-$10.

Volume 10, "Mr. Lisa Goes to Washington"/"When Flanders Failed," 1999. Fox Video. Includes short "Burp Contest" from "The Tracey Ullman Show." Also sold as part of a three-cassette box set with volumes 11 and 12. Sealed. . . . .$5-$10 for single, $15-$25 for box set.

Volume 11, "Bart the Murderer"/"Like Father, Like Clown," 1999. Fox Video. Includes "Grandpa & The Kids" from "The Tracey Ullman Show." Sealed. . . . .$5-$10.

Volume 12, "Treehouse of Horror II (The Simpsons Halloween Special)"/"Lisa's Pony," 1999. Fox Video. Includes short "Making Faces" from "The Tracey Ullman Show." Sealed. $5-$10.

CDs, tapes and vinyl

Audio cassette, "The Simpsons Sing the Blues," 1990. Geffen. 1. "Do the Bartman," 2. "School Day," 3. "Born Under a Bad Sign," 4. "Moanin' Lisa Blues," 5. "Deep, Deep Trouble," 6. "God Bless The Child," 7. "I Love to See You Smile," 8. "Springfield Soul Stew," 9. "Look At All Those Idiots," and 10. "Sibling Rivalry." Sealed. . . . .$5-$10.

"The Simpsons Sing the Blues" compact disc long box, 1990, Geffen Records. Punch along perforations on back for stand-up Bart.

Compact discs: "The Simpsons Sing the Blues," "Songs in the Key of Springfield," "Yellow Album," "Deep, Deep Trouble" single, "Do the Bartman" single and "Do the Bartman" single with flip book.

Audio cassette, "The Simpsons: Songs in the Key of Springfield: Original Music From The Television Series," 1997. Rhino Records. Sealed. . . . .$5-$12.

Audio cassette, "The Yellow Album," 1998. Geffen. Cover of album is a parody of the Beatles' "Sgt. Pepper" album. 1. "Love?" 2. "Sisters Are Doin' It For Themselves," 3. "Funny How Time Slips Away," 4. "Twenty-Four Hours A Day," 5. "The Ten Commandments Of Bart," 6. "I Just Can't Help Myself, 7. "She's Comin' Out Swingin'," 8. "Anyone Else," 9. "Every Summer With You" and 10. "Hail To Thee, Kamp Krusty." Sealed. . . . .$7-$12.

Compact disc album, "The Simpsons Sing the Blues," 1990. Same cuts as audio cassette. Geffen. Sealed. . . . .$7-$15.

Compact disc album, "The Simpsons: Songs in the Key of Springfield: Original Music from the Television Series." Same cuts as the cassette but with more liner-notes information. . . . . . .$7-$16.

Compact disc album, "Music for a Darkened Theater," 1990. Danny Elfman, Geffen. Disc features Simpsons theme song. Sealed. . . . . $5-$10.

Compact disc album, "The Yellow Album," 1998. Geffen. Cover of album is a parody of the Beatles' "Sgt. Pepper" album. Same cuts as cassette. Sealed. . . . .$10-$15.

Compact disc maxi-single, "Deep Deep Trouble" (three versions) and "Sibling Rivalry," 1991. Geffen. (21633). Gatefold hardcover with sticker that reads: "Punch out along perforations for your standup Bart and Homer 'Deep, Deep Trouble Portrait.' Totally unsuitable for framing, man!" Sealed. .$15-$25.

Compact disc single, "Do the Bartman," 1991. Geffen. (GEF87CD). "Bad Bart House Mix," "A capella," "7-inch House Mix/Edit" and "LP Edit." . . . .$15.

"The Simpsons Sing the Blues" vinyl album, 1990, Geffen Records. 33 rpm.

Compact disc single, "Do the Bartman," 1991. Geffen (PRO-CD-4170). "7-inch House Mix/Edit," "LP Edit," "Bad Bart House Mix," "Swingin' in the House Mix," "LP Version," and "A capella." Folder-type packaging includes 4-by-4-inch flip book. Sealed. . . . .$30-$45.

Compact disc single, "Deep, Deep Trouble," 1991. Geffen. (GEF88CD). "Full Dance Mix," "LP Edit," "Dance Mix Edit" and "Springfield Soul Stew." . . . .$15.

Compact disc single, "Deep, Deep Trouble" (four versions), 1991. Geffen (PRO-CD-4208). "Edit," "Dance Mix Edit," "LP Version," and "Full Dance Mix." Sealed. . . . .$7-$15.

Compact disc single, "God Bless The Child," 1991. Geffen. (PRO-CD-4218). . . . .$10.

7-inch vinyl single, "Do the Bartman," 1991. Geffen. (GEF87). "7-inch House Mix/Edit" and "Edit." . . . .$10.

7-inch vinyl single, "Deep, Deep Trouble," 1991. Geffen. (GEF88). "Dance Mix Edit" and "LP Edit." . . . .$10.

12-inch vinyl single, "Do the Bartman," 1991. Geffen. (GEF87T). "Bad Bart House Mix (A capella)" and "Swingin' in the House." . .$20.

12-inch vinyl single, "Deep, Deep Trouble," 1991. Geffen. (GEF88T). "Full Dance Mix, "LP Edit" and "Springfield Soul Stew." . . . .$20.

12-inch vinyl single, "Deep, Deep Trouble," 1991. Geffen. (PRO-A-4226). "Full Dance Mix," "LP Version," "Dance Mix Edit," and "Edit." . . . .$12.

Picture disc, "Deep, Deep Trouble." Vinyl disc shaped like Bart singing with a microphone, 1991. Geffen. (GEF88P). "Dance Mix Edit" and "LP Edit" .$35.

Vinyl album, "Simpsons Sing the Blues," 1990. Geffen. 33 rpm. Same cuts as compact disc and cassette. Sealed. . . . .$20-$35.

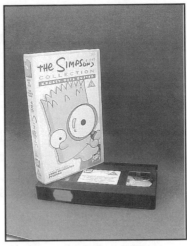

British home video of "Krusty Gets Busted" and "Some Enchanted Evening," 1997, Fox Video U.K. The cassette is compatible only with the PAL video system widely used in Europe.

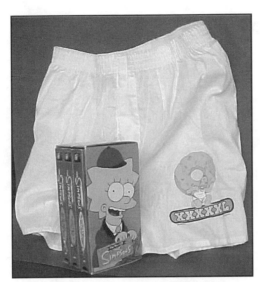

Fox Home Video gave away these Homer Simpson boxer shorts in 1999 with the purchase of the Wave 4 box set (volumes 10, 11 and 12). Despite the design on the front indicating these are Homer-sized extra-extra-extra-extra-extra large shorts, the pair is medium-sized for waists 34 to 36 inches.

German cassette from Karussell featuring audio translations for the Simpsons episodes "Bart Gets Hit By a Car," translated here as "Bart kommt unter die Rader." and "One Fish, Two Fish, Blowfish, Blue Fish," translated as "Die 24-Stunden-Frist." German fans could play the cassette while watching the original English version of the show.

Three Simpsons phone cards, 1995, Frontier. Each card, now expired, offered $10 of long-distance domestic phone calls. Users could also, according to packaging, "send a zany wake-up call from Bart himself (fun for you and your friends)." And the cards featured "personal 24-hour voice mail ... and much, more more."

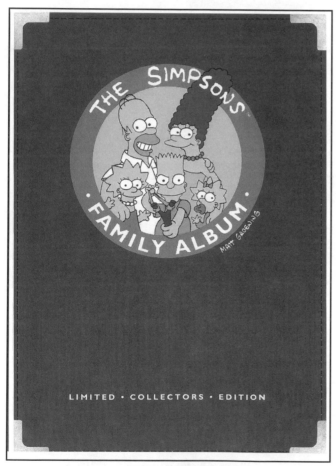

The Simpsons Family Album phone card, 1994, PACS. Australia. This limited-edition card, with $5 worth of phone service, is sealed inside this colorful 8¼-by-12-inch plastic folder.

Personalized Bart greeting card, 1997, American Greetings. Text on the card reads: "(Receiver), this is a way-cool birthday card! ... Cause it's for someone way-cool!" This card was created at an American Greetings video kiosk. These screens are often found in grocery stores and card shops.

19 Cards

Greeting cards

Gibson

BG040-2371, Bart, 1995. "There are two things that I want you know. 1. We'll be friends forever. 2. Cross me, man, and I'll drop you like a bad habit." . . . .$3.

BG040-2363, Lisa, 1995. "A birthday is a sobering time, when the impact of the lost potential of your life becomes almost tangible. How sad that you never paint a masterpiece, write that Pulitzer-winning novel, invent the cheap, clean power source of the future, or, even be noticed by more than a fraction of the population. Happy birthday, if you feel that's appropriate." . . . .$3.

BG040-2336, Lisa, 1995. "Another birthday? Looks like someone's got the cake's-flamin', time's-flyin', skin's-wrinklin', butt's-droopin', hair's graying', memory's-going', talkin'-to-myself 'cause-I-ain't-as-young as-I-used-to-be, noddin'-off blues." . . . .$3.

BG040-2368, Grandpa, 1995. "No matter how old I get ... you'll always be older than me! Happy birthday." . . . .$3.

BG040-2369, Marge, 1995. "We're such good friends that I consider you a member of the family. Please don't be insulted." . . . .$3.

BG040-2390, Baby Bart, 1995. "Good good ga loo ga la! Translation: 'Here comes your birthday cake via airmail, man!' Happy birthday." . . . . .$3.

M600-0324, Bart, 1995. "Hey, sis, I was gonna give you the coolest birthday gift, the one that really keeps on giving ... but Mom said, No tattoos! Happy birthday anyway." . . . .$3.

F00768, Homer, Bart, Lisa and Maggie, 1994. "And they said radiation makes you sterile. Happy Father's Day." . . . .$4.

F02769, Homer and Bart, 1995. "To the man who taught me how to live life to its fullest. Happy Father's Day." . . . .$4.

NP200-0300, Mr. Burns, 1994. "Happy birthday. Now get back to work. (This personal birthday sentiment has been brought to you by the Springfield Nuclear Power Plant. Providing safe, clean and efficient energy for a happy, healthy, and productive company.) Your pay will be docked for the time it took to read this card." . . . .$4.

NP200-0301, Apu, 1994. "I am not meaning to suggest that you are old ... but when is the last time you have been checked for the expiration date, please?" . . . .$4.

NP200-0302, Grandpa, 1994. "Not bad for someone with the life expectancy of a moth. Happy birthday." . . . .$4.

NP200-0303, Otto, 1994. "Remember when your old man said you'd never amount to anything? He was wrong, man! Just one checkmark on the back of your driver's license and you're spare parts for ten people." . . . .$4.

V01894, Homer Valentine, 1995. "You're cuter than a bowling ball, you're smarter than a cruller, just like a floor without its wax, without you I'd be duller." . . . .$3.

X03998, Marge (with hair decorated like a Christmas tree), 1994. "Merry Christmas." . . .$4.

Pocket No. 7, Lisa, 1995. "Are you too smart for your own good? Does the conformity of antiquated gender stereotyping bore you? Do you suspect that the fashion industry exists solely for the amusement of extraterrestrials? Welcome to the club." . . . .$3.

Simpsons greeting cards, 1991 & 1995, Gibson Greetings.

Greeting cards: No stamps required

In the U.S., American Greetings sells Simpsons cards at thousands of video kiosks in grocery stores, card shops and other places. Buyers touch the video screen a few times to select the style of card ("The Simpsons" is just one option), type in the name of the recipient, then stare as a pen magically zips around a piece of heavy-duty card stock. In about 10 minutes, you've got a personalized, colorful greeting card for about $3 to $4.

American Greetings' Web site (www.americangreetings.com) offers an online version it will print and send to the recipient by first-class mail. One Simpsons selection is a hilarious Homer all-occasion card for $3.50. The cover reads: "You know, (Receiver), great minds think alike ..." The inside verse adds: "Does your butt itch, too?"

Not long ago, American Greetings launched Greet Mail, allowing buyers to order cards delivered through e-mail. For those looking to spread the word about the fun of owning Simpsons merchandise, what could be better than cards that instantly turn others into Simpsons collectors?

Pocket No. 8, Lisa, 1995. "Sorry. For a second there, I pictured not having you as a friend." . .$3.

Pocket No. 9, Homer, 1995. "Love is like fried pork chops. Except of course, pork chops are tastier." . . . .$3.

Pocket No. 16, Homer, 1995. "D'Oh! I can't believe I forgot your birthday. Hope it was happy." . . . .$3.

Pocket No. 17, Mr. Burns and Smithers, 1995. "I can't believe the things you make me do for you. Don't ever change." . . . .$3.

Pocket No. 18, Otto, 1995. "It's like so cool to have someone you can relate to on a really deep level. No one else understands me the way you do. So, like, how long did you spend in the wacky tank?" . . . .$3.

Pocket No. 25, Otto, 1995. "You better groove on my present, 'cause, like, it's s'posed to make a lasting impression." . . . .$3.

Pocket No. 26, Grandpa, 1995. "Take it from me. The ol' memory's the first thing to go. Take it from me. The ol' memory's the first thing to go." . . . .$3.

Pocket No. 27, Bart, 1995. "There are two things I want you to know: 1. We'll be friends forever and ever. 2. Cross me, man, and I'll drop you like a bad habit. Happy birthday." . . . .$3.

Pocket No. 31, Lisa, 1991. "Don't worry about another birthday! You're just as immature as ever." . . . .$4.

Pocket No. 32, Bart, 1991. "You'll be getting a lot of attention today. Don't get too used to it. Happy birthday!" . . . .$4.

Pocket No. 33, Homer, 1991. "Another birthday? What a hair raising experience!" . . . .$4.

Pocket No. 34, Bart, 1991. "A few simple words of advice, as you travel down the road of life. ... Act your age, not your shoe size, man! Happy Birthday." . . . .$4.

Pocket No. 34, Devil, 1995. "Another year's gone by and you haven't aged a day. Now why don't you make it official by signing on the dotted line? Enjoy the day ... if you can." . . . .$3.

Pocket No. 35, Bart, 1991. "Warning: Do not attempt this trick at home. The manufacturers of this card will not be held responsible for candle wax burns, broken gifts or stained carpeting. Happy birthday!" . . . .$4.

Pocket No. 35, Skinner, 1995. "I hope you realize there's more to your birthday than the weary humor of a few novelty gifts and the empty well-wishing of indifferent co-workers. By golly, there's cake." . . . .$3.

Pocket No. 36, Bart, 1991. "Yo, man! This year I got you the present you've always dreamed of ... and then I woke up! Happy birthday." . . . .$4.

Pocket No. 36, Moleman, 1995. "For your birthday I got you a one-of-a-kind gift: Something very stimulating and well within my price range. ME." . . . .$3.

Pocket No. 37, Bart, 1991. "Live for the presents, man! Happy birthday!" . . . .$4.

Pocket No. 38, Maggie 1991. "Getting older sucks! But have a happy birthday anyway!" . .$4.

Pocket No. 39, family, 1991. "Say cheese!" (Homer) "Cheese!"(Marge) "Cheese!" (Lisa) "Cheese Log!" (Bart). "You always were a little different. Happy Birthday!" . . . .$4.

Pocket No. 40, Homer, 1991. "Eat, drink and be merry, for tomorrow we diet — Homer Simpson." . . . .$4.

Pocket No. 41, Lisa, 1991. "You've filled my life with love, music and meaning! So how about some money? You forgot money!" . . . .$4.

Pocket No. 42, Bart, 1991. "I feel close to you." . . . .$4.

Pocket No. 43, Bart, 1991. "It's scary, I know ... to have a friend like me." . . . .$4.

Pocket No. 44, Bart, 1991. "Food fight ... You're askin' for it, man! The worst thing about getting older is discovering your conscience. Happy birthday, anyway." . . . .$4.

Pocket No. 44, Mr. Burns, 1995. "Happy birthday. Now get back to work." . . . .$3.

Pocket No. 45, Bart, 1991. "How many fingers am I holding up? If your answer was two, you're not celebrating enough! Happy birthday!" . . . .$4.

Pocket No. 45, Flanders, 1995. "Okely dokely dee! Here's a greeting from me. Okely Dokely Dum! Can you guess who it's from? Okely dokely doo! Happy birthday to you!" . . . .$3.

Pocket No. 46, Marge and Homer, 1991. "Of all the things I adore about you, one quality stands out in my mind. ... You get more squeezable every year! Happy birthday!" . . . .$4.

American Greetings

2306343, Simpsons family, 1997. "We wouldn't say there are too many candles on your cake. We'd say ... Stop! It's blinding me with its radiance! Quick! Someone call the fire department! Ow! My hair's on fire! Aye carumba! Suck! Suck! Suck!" . . . .$3.

2306351, Homer, 1997. "A special birthday wish from Homer and me ... Hmphmphy Burrphday!" . . . .$3.

2456016, Bart, 1997. "I wanted to get you the perfect birthday present ... But how do you wrap a wedgie?" . . . .$3.

FV0176-05A, Homer and Marge, 1997. "Y'know, lots of women marry a guy, and then try to change him, but not me. I love you just the way you are. But don't get any worse! Love You. Happy Valentine's Day." . . . .$4.

Carlton Cards

2183069, Bart, 1997. "I wanted to get you the perfect present ... But how do you wrap a wedgie?" . . . .$3.

2306326, Bart, 1997. "If you take life one day at a time, those days turn into weeks, weeks turn into months, months turn into years, and before you know it ... You're dead. (Hang in there.)" . . . .$3.

2306332, Bart, 1997. "Aye, carumba! Sometimes a good 'Aye, carumba' can help you through the day!" . . . .$3.

Wallet cards

Simpsons 3-by-2-inch wallet cards, 1990 & 1992, Legends of Entertainment and O.S.P Publishing.

Bart, "Don't have a cow, man!" 1990. Legends of Entertainment. . . . .$3.

Bart, "Outta my way, man!" 1990. Legends of Entertainment. . . . .$3.

Bartman, "Identify yourself, man!" 1990. Legends of Entertainment. . . . .$3.

Itchy and Scratchy, meat grinder, 1992. O.S.P.

Publishing. Front shows mouse putting cat through meat grinder. . . . .$3.

Itchy and Scratchy, red hots, 1992. O.S.P. Publishing. Front shows mouse giving a mustard-laden firecracker in a bun to the cat. . . . .$3.

Itchy and Scratchy, blender, 1992. O.S.P. Publishing. Front shows the cat caught in a kitchen blender. Back shows mouse with a milk shake full of cat's body parts. . . . .$3.

Krusty Flakes cereal box, 1992. O.S.P. Publishing. Front shows Krusty the Clown on cereal box, Krusty Flakes. . . . .$3.

Lisa playing saxophone, 1990. Legends of Entertainment. Front shows Lisa playing saxophone, which has musical notes coming from it. . . . .$3.

Maggie, "Suck, Suck, Suck," 1990. Legends of Entertainment. Front shows Maggie on skateboard. . . . .$3.

Family, posing, 1990. Legends of Entertainment. . . . .$3.

Phone cards

Bart, 1995. Frontier. He is happily taking his time making a phone call in a booth while angry eyes of unknown others look in. . . . .$3-$10.

Family, 1995. Frontier. A ringing telephone is lost in Marge's hair while other family members look for it. . . . .$3-$5.

Homer, 1995. Frontier. He is tangled in telephone cord while he's on the phone. . . . .$3-$5.

The Simpsons Family Album, 1994. PACS. Australia. "Limited collectors edition." Sealed in plastic in an 8¼-by-12-inch folder. . . . .$25.

Bart Simpson "Don't have a cow, man!" post card, 1990, Classico San Francisco Inc. 4 by 6 inches.

Post cards

Bart, "Don't have a cow, man!" 1990. Classico San Francisco. 4 by 6 inches. . . . .$3.

Bart, "No way, man!" 1990. Classico San Francisco. 4 by 6 inches. . . . .$3.

Family, "A Complete Guide" book promo, 1997. Bongo. 6 by 4½ inches. . . . .$5.

Homer chasing Bart, Animation. Promo for animation show. . . . .$3.

Radioactive Man, 1994. Bongo Comics. 7 by 5 inches. Radioactive Man lifts a plate with the Simpsons on it. . . . .$4.

Bart Simpson "No way, man!" post card, 1990, Classico San Francisco Inc. 4 by 6 inches.

Trading cards

Downunder, 1996. Tempo. Australia. 100-card set. "Full bleed" series with seven cards per foil pack. Subsets: Character cards, Bart vs. Australia, Tour of Springfield, Zombie and Blackboard Puzzle. Insert cards and quantities of each: "Homer As ..." (7) 1:9 packets; "The Seven Duffs" (7) — die-cut polycards 1:30 packets; "Springfield's Finest" (4) — polycards 1:65 packets; "Redemption Card" (1) — America's Most Nuclear Family 1:360 packets; Bartarang" (1) 1:9,000 packets. Sealed packs: $3. Individual cards: 50 cents.

Skybox Series I, 1994. Skybox. 36 packs (8 cards per pack). $45 for sealed box, $2 per pack, $10 for full set of 80 cards, 10 cents for each card. Insert cards and quantities of each: "Wiggle" (9), $3 each; "Cels" (6), $5 each; "Glow in the Dark" (4), $7 each; "Art Bart Redemption Card" (400 made), $150 each.

Skybox Series II, 1994. Skybox. 36 packs (8 cards per pack), $30 for sealed box, $1 per pack, $10 for full set of 80 cards, 10 cents for each card. Insert cards: "Smell-O-Rama" (10), $2 each; "Disappearing Ink" (4), $7 each; "Wiggle" (9), $4 each; "Arty Art" (4), $30 each.

Skybox card tin, 1994. Skybox. 4½-inch-high red, metal tin to hold Simpsons cards. Premium for sending in Skybox card wrappers. (Offer expired.) . . . .$25.

Topps Series box, 8-card packs, 1990. Topps. 36 packs (8 cards and 1 sticker per pack). Wrapper is waxed paper. Cards are glossy on one side. $15 for box. .$1 per pack, $8 for full set of 88 cards, 22 stickers.

Topps Series box, 16-card packs, 1990. Topps. 24 packs (16 cards and one sticker per pack). Similar to eight-card packs, except there are twice as many cards per pack. Wrapper is cellophane. $20 for complete box, $2 per pack, $8 for full set of 88 cards with 22 stickers.

Simpsons Downunder trading cards and wrapper, 1996, Tempo. Australia. Glossy stock, high-quality art and clever writing.

Simpsons Topps trading cards, 1990, Topps. Display box reads: "Exotic cards! Annoying stickers! Bewildering puzzles! And fun galore!"

Simpsons Skybox Series II trading cards and wrapper, 1994, Skybox. Insert cards include Smell-O-Rama, Disappearing Ink, Wiggle and Arty Art.

20 Holiday and party

Halloween

Costume, Bart reading book, 1989. Ben Cooper. Plastic Bart mask and an orange-blue full-body garment. Boxed. . . . .$10-$20.

Costume, Bart holding bag, 1989. Ben Cooper. Plastic Bart mask and light blue polyester-nylon full-body garment. Boxed. . . . .$10-$20.

Costume, Bart on skateboard, 1989. Ben Cooper. Plastic Bart mask and orange-and-blue full-body garment. Boxed. . . . .$10-$20.

Costume, Bart with slingshot, 1990. Norben Products. Canada. Full-length vinyl costume with cardboard mask. Carded. . . . .$15-$25.

Costume, Lisa, "Oh, brother!" 1989. Ben Cooper. Plastic Lisa mask and orange polyester-nylon waist-length garment. Boxed. . . . .$10-$20.

Mask, vinyl, Bart, 1989. Ben Cooper. Yellow mask of Bart that wraps around the head. Bagged. . . . .$30-$40.

Mask, vinyl, Marge. Large yellow mask of Marge that wraps around the head.$60.

Mask, plastic, Marge, 1989. Ben Cooper. Yellow and blue face mask with rubber band. . . . .$7.

Mask, vinyl, Homer. Large yellow mask of Homer that wraps around the head. . . . .$60.

Mask, plastic, Homer, 1989. Ben Cooper. Yellow face mask with rubber band. . . . .$7.

Mask, plastic, Bart, 1989. Ben Cooper. Yellow face mask with rubber band. . . . .$5.

Mask, plastic, Lisa, 1989. Ben Cooper. Yellow face mask with rubber band. . . . .$5.

Poncho, Bart, "Boo, man!," 1991, Norben. Canada. Plastic poncho for a child to wear as costume. Sealed. . . . .$5-$15.

Full-size Homer and Marge Simpson vinyl masks, early 1990s.

Christmas

Ornament, Bart, 1998. Carlton Cards. 3½-inch hard-plastic figure of Bart in a Santa cap and carrying presents on his skateboard. Display box reads: "Cowabunga! Bart's one bad boy, on a mission from Santa to spread Christmas joy." Boxed. . . . .$7-$15.

Ornament, family members hanging on candy canes. Bagged. . . . .$2-$6 each.

Ornament, Homer, 1999. Carlton Cards. 4-inch hard-plastic figure of Homer in Santa suit as he rings bell and holds a can of Duff beer. Display box reads: "With his cheesy fake beard and protruding beer gut, Homer Simpson is anything but the classic Santa of Christmas legend." Boxed. . . . . .10-$16.

Valentine's Day

Cards, 38-count, 1994. Cleo. 35 student cards, one teacher card, two bonus cards on back of box, and non-mailable envelopes. Boxed. . . . .$3-$10.

Cards, 34-count, 1998. Carlton Cards. 30 student cards, four teacher cards, and non-mailable envelopes. Boxed. . . . . . .$2-$7.

Cards, 34-count, 1997. American Greetings. 32 student cards, two teacher cards, and non-mailable envelopes. Boxed. . . . .$2-$7.

Cards, 32-count, 1994. Cleo. 31 student cards, one teacher card, two bonus cards on back of box, and non-mailable envelopes. . . . .$3-$10.

Simpsons boxed Valentine cards, 34-count, 1997, American Greetings. Includes two teacher cards.

Stickers, family, 1994. Cleo. Four-sheet pack with nine stickers per sheet. Sealed. . . . .$2-$5.

Hats, family, 1990. Partytime. Canada. 6 cone-shaped paper party hats with elastic chin straps. Sealed. . . . .$3-$5.

Birthday parties, etc.

Bags, "Happy birthday," Bart, Lisa and Maggie, 1990. Party Creations. Eight party bags. Sealed. . . . .$2-$5.

Bags, Bart, "Happy birthday, dude!" 1990. Partytime. Canada. 12 loot bags. Packaging also says, "Bonne Fete, mon chum!" Sealed. . . . .$2-$5.

Blowouts, Bart, "Cowabunga!" 1990. Partytime. Canada. Six party blowouts. Sealed. . . . .$3-$7.

Cake decoration, Bart, Lisa and Maggie, "Happy birthday," 1990. Wilton. 5½-inch-diameter paper used to top cakes. Sealed. . . . .$1-$4.

Cake decorating kit, "Happy birthday," 1990. Wilton. Kit includes paper cake decoration and detailed instructions. Sealed. . . . . .$3-$7.

Candle and cake decoration, family, 1990. Wilton. Five candles shaped like the Simpsons. Carded. . . . .$3-$7.

Candle and cake decoration, Maggie, 1st birthday, 1990. Wilton. 3-inch-high candle showing Maggie hugging a No. 1. Carded. . . . .$2-$5.

Cake pan, Bart, "Happy birthday, man!" 1990. Wilton. 14-inch metal cake pan molded to look like Bart from waist up. Tagged. . . . .$8.

Cups, Bart and Homer, "Happy birthday," 1990. Partytime. Canada. Six foam cups. "Happy birthday" is written in English and French. Sealed. . . . .$2-$5.

Cups, Bart and Lisa, 1989. Chesapeake Consumer Products Co. Eight 9-oz., plastic-lined paper cups. Lisa is chasing Bart. Sealed. . .$2-$5.

Gift bag, Baby Bart, 1994. Gibson Greetings. 10 inches high. Design shows Baby Bart tossing food with spoon. Tagged. . . . .$2-$5.

Gift wrap, 1-sheet party. Rainbow Star. Canada. 27-by-40-inch sheet. Design shows Simpsons characters and party foods. Sealed. . . . .$2-$5.

Simpsons blowouts, 1990, Partytime. Canada. six party noise-makers, each showing Bart saying "Cowabunga!"

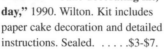

Bart Simpson cake pan, 1990, Wilton. Packaging reads: "Pan takes any 2-layer cake mix. Suggested tips, colors and instructions on back of label."

Maggie Simpson first-birthday candle and cake decoration, 1990, Wilton. 3-inch high candle.

Simpsons "Party Down" invitations, Party Creations. Inside has room to write invitation instructions.

Invitations, "Party!" 1995. Gibson. 8 party invitations. Front shows Bart and handwritten sign: "Party! No dorks allowed." Inside the invitation it reads: "But I'll make an exception in your case." Sealed. . . . . .$2-$5.

Invitations, "It's a party!" Party Creations. Eight party invitations. Front shows family dancing and Bart saying, "Be there or be square, man!" Sealed. . . . .$3-$7.

Invitations, "Party down!" Party Creations. Eight party invitations. Front shows Bart, Lisa and Maggie and "Party down!" Sealed. . . . .$3-$7.

Napkins, beverage, Bart, Lisa and Maggie, "Party down, man!" 1989, Chesapeake Consumer Products Co. Package of 24. Sealed. . . . .$3-$5.

Napkins, luncheon, Bart, Lisa and Maggie, "Party down, man!" 1989. Chesapeake Consumer Products Co. Package of 24. Sealed. . . . .$3-5.

Simpsons party plates, 1990, Party Creations and Chesapeake Consumer Products Company.

Napkins, luncheon, family dancing, "The Simpsons Party!" 1989. Chesapeake Consumer Products Co. Package of 24. Sealed. . . . . . .$3-$5.

Napkins, luncheon, Bart, "Happy birthday," 1990. Partytime. Canada. Package of 16. Sealed. . . . .$5-$8.

Plates, 7-inch, Bart, "Happy birthday," 1990. Partytime. Canada. Six 7-inch paper plates. "Happy birthday. Bonne fette." Sealed. . . . .$2-$5.

Plates, 7-inch, Bart, Lisa, and Maggie, "Happy birthday," 1989. Chesapeake Consumer Products Co. Eight 7-inch paper plates. Sealed. . . . .$2-$5.

Plates, 7-inch, family dancing. Party Creations. Sealed. . . . .$2-$5.

Plates, 9-inch, Bart, Lisa and Maggie, 1989, Chesapeake Consumer Products Co. Eight 9-inch paper plates. Sealed. . . . .$3-$6.

Plates, 9-inch, family dancing. Party Creations. Sealed. . . . .$3-$6.

Tablecover, Bart, Lisa and Maggie, 1990. Chesapeake Consumer Products Co. 54-by-96-inch plastic. Sealed. . . . .$2-$7.

Tablecover, party foods, 1990. Partytime. Canada. 54-by-96-inch plastic showing Simpsons characters and party foods. Sealed. . . . .$2-$7.

Watch favors, Bart, 1990. Partytime. Canada. Tiny games that look like real watches. Roll metal beads into holes. Carded. . . . .$4-$10.

Yo-yo favors, Bart, 1990. Partytime. Canada. Six 1-inch-diameter yo-yos. Carded. . . . .$2-$7.

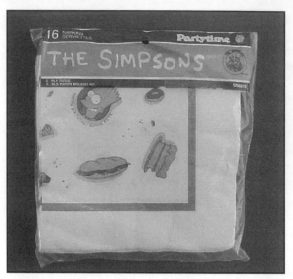

"Happy birthday" luncheon napkins, 1990, Partytime. Canada. Package of 16 napkins, each featuring a design with Bart Simpson and various party foods.

"Party down, man!" beverage napkins, 1989, Chesapeake Consumer Products Co. Package of 24 napkins, each featuring a design with Lisa, Maggie and Bart Simpson.

Homer Simpson lunch bags, 1990, The Fern Group Limited. Originally sold in Canada, this package of 25 lunch bags show Homer with an apron that reads, "Kiss the chef."

21 Miscellaneous

Banks

Simpsons tin bank, 1995, Dalson. Australia. 10 inches high. Design shows family members racing in a car next to a sign that says, "Moe's Last Chance Diner." The other side shows Bart leaning against a gas pump that says, "Gasso Petroleum Gasoline."

Simpsons plastic key rings, 1989 & 1990, Button-Up. Each is about 2 by 1¾ inches.

Bart 10-inch-high figure, 1990. Street Kids. Variations include green shirt and light blue pants. Boxed. . . . .$5-$10.

Butterfinger, Bart figure, 1990. Street Kids. 13-inch-high yellow plastic in the shape of Bart's body. Originally filled with Butterfinger Fun Size bars. Sealed. . . . .$10-$20.

Butterfinger tin, Bart as pirate, 1992. Perugina Brands of America. Boxed-shaped candy tin. Originally filled with Butterfinger Fun Size bars. Sealed. . . . .$12-$18.

Family traveling tin, 1995. Dalson. Australia. 10-inch-high circular tin with coin slot on top. . . . .$12.

Gumball machine, Bart, 1990. Jolly Good Industries. 6½ inches high with clear, bubble-shaped plastic gumball holder. Boxed. . . . .$20-$35.

Gumball machine, Maggie and Lisa, 1990. Jolly Good Industries. 6½ inches high with clear, bubble-shaped plastic gumball holder. Boxed. . . . .$30-$40.

Balloons

5-pack, family, 1990. National Latex Products Co. Five 14-inch balloons. Bagged. . . . . . .$2-$5.

Bart Simpson coin bank with Butterfinger candy bars, 1990. Street Kids. Stickers form eyes, shirt and pants. Bank originally stuffed with tiny candy bars.

12-pack, family, 1990. Partytime. Bagged. . . . .$2-$5.

Mylar, family, 1990. 18-inch diameter. M&D Balloons. Simpsons with the words, "Get Well or We'll Come." . . . .$2-$7.

Mylar, Bartman, 1990. M&D Balloons. 18-inch diameter. Bartman saying "Watch it, dude." . . . . .$2-$7.

Mylar, Bart on skateboard, 1990. M&D Balloons. 18-inch diameter. Bart riding on skateboard saying, "Go for it, man!" . . . .$2-$7.

Mylar, Marge and Homer, 1990. M&D Balloons. 18-inch diameter. Marge and Homer hugging, along with the words, "You Know I Love You." . . . .$2-$7.

Punch, Homer and Bart, 1990. National Latex Products Co. Variations include blue and pink. Sealed. . . . .$2-$5.

Key rings

Button-Up

Bart, "Aye carumba!" 1990. 2-by-1¼-inch clear plastic. . . . .$4.

Bart, "Cool your jets, man!" 1990. 2-by-1¼-inch clear plastic. . . . .$4.

How a key ring made the big screen

Bart Simpson makes a quick cameo in the 1992 film "Basic Instinct." Watch carefully. You might miss him.

Michael Douglas plays homicide detective Nick Curran. Sharon Stone is Catherine Tramell, a suspect in a bizarre sex-related homicide. Nick finds himself deeply attracted to her, even as he conducts the murder investigation.

Script writer Joe Eszterhas reportedly earned $3 million for his screenplay, but at least one detail was left to the (more modestly paid) prop people. Near the end of the film, Nick confronts the believed killer in a hallway.

As the suspect reaches into one of the pockets of her raincoat, apparently to pull a gun, Nick shoots and kills her. But when he checks the pocket, there's no weapon. It's only a set of keys on a ring attached to a 3-inch-high PVC figure of Bart Simpson. Oops.

California graphic-design expert Phillip Franklin, a longtime Simpsons fan, says he has a friend who worked on props for the film. It was her idea to borrow Franklin's Bart key chain for the scene.

"She was involved in movie props and needed a big enough key chain. I gave the Bart key chain to her. That's the last I saw of it until it appeared on camera for about one-half second," Franklin says. "It was never returned."

But the story has a happy ending. Franklin in 1986 posted a note on the Internet seeking to buy another Bart key ring, and found one right away.

Bart, "Don't have a cow, man!" 1989. 2-by-1¼-inch clear plastic.. . . . .$4.

Bart, "Fun has a name & it's Bartholomew J. Simpson," 1990. 2-by-1¼-inch clear plastic. . . . .$4.

Bart, "Gangway, man!" 1990. 2-by-1¼-inch clear plastic. . . . .$4.

Bart, "I'm Bart Simpson. Who the hell are you?" 1990. 2-by-1¼-inch. . . . .$4.

Bart, "Yo, man!" 1989. 2-by-1¼-inch clear plastic. . . . . . .$4.

Bart, "B. Simpson Esquire," 1990. 2-by-1¼-inch clear plastic. . . . .$4.

Bart, "Underachiever," 1989. 2-by-1¼-inch clear plastic. $4.

Bartman, "Watch it, dude!" 1989. 2-by-1¼-inch clear plastic. . . . .$4.

Family on couch, 1989. 2-by-1¼-inch clear plastic. . . . .$4.

Family, posing, 1989. 2-by-1¼-inch clear plastic. . . . .$4.

Family, standing together lovingly, 1989. 2-by-1¼-inch clear plastic. . . . .$4.

Homer, "No problemo," 1989. 2-by-1¼-inch clear plastic. $4.

Bart Simpson PVC key ring, 1990, Street Kids. 3 inches high.

Bart Simpson key ring, 1997, Vivid Imaginations. U.K. Pictured with display card.

Gift Creations

Bart "Right-on, dude," 1990. Metal. . . . .$4.

Bart and Homer, "Why you little —!" 1990. Circular metal. 1¾ inches in diameter." . . . . . .$4.

Family posing, 1990. Metal. . . . .$4.

Other

Family posing, PVC, 1990. Molded yellow plastic. . . . .$3.

Bart PVC figural, 1990. Street Kids. 3 inches high. Variations include light-blue shirt, dark-blue shirt, orange shirt and red shirt. Carded. . . .$2-$5.

Bart making a face, 1997. Vivid Imaginations. U.K. 2¼-by-2¼ inches. Carded. . . . .$2-$4.

Homer holding Duff Beer, 1997. Vivid Imaginations. U.K. 2¼-by-3 inches. Carded.$2-$4.

Homer and Marge hugging, 1997. Vivid Imaginations. U.K. 2¼-by-3 inches. Carded. Sealed. . . . .$2-$4.

Watches

Nelsonic

Bart, "Don't have a cow, man!" 1990. Variations: 8-inch blue band and 9½-inch black band with a slightly larger watch face. Flip-up cover over digital display. Carded. . . .$5-$12.

Bartman, "Avenger of Evil," 1990. Variations: 8-inch black band and 9½-inch blue band with a slightly larger watch face. Flip-up cover over digital display. Carded. . . . .$5-$12.

Family dancing, 1990. Variations: 8-inch blue band and 9½-inch black band with slightly larger watch face. Flip-up cover over digital display. . . . .$5-$12.

Bart Simpson "Don't have a cow, man!" watch, 1990, Nelsonic. Digital display with flip-top cover over dial.

Itchy (the mouse) & Scratchy (the cat)

Barbershop scene, 1993. Big-Time. Carded. . . . .$7-$20.

Sitting at a table, 1993. Big-Time. Carded. . . . .$7-$20.

Eating hot dogs, 1993. Big-Time. Carded. . . . .$7-$20.

14 different animation cels on the band, 1992. Big-Time. Carded. . . . .$7-$20.

Other

Bart and Lisa, "Get out of my face, man," 1990. Today Products. Canada. Analog with sweep second hand. Blue plastic strap. Boxed. . . . .$15-$25.

Bart, "Don't have a cow, man!" 1990. Today Products. Canada. Analog with sweep second

hand. Workings visible inside. Clear plastic strap. Boxed. . . . .$15-$25.

Bart, "Who do I look like, Father Time?" 1990. Analog with sweep second hand. . . . .$25.

Bart, "Aye, carumba," 1997. Wesco. U.K. Boxed. . . . .$10-$25.

Butterfinger, 1990. Nestles. Analog watch with sweep second hand. Face shows Butterfinger candy bar at top, with heads of Bart, Maggie and Lisa circling the dial. Bagged. . . . .$25-$35.

Family, 1990. Today Products. Canada. Analog with sweep second hand. Leather band. Boxed. . . . .$25-$35.

Bart Subway hologram, 1997. Subway sandwich restaurants. Digital watch with black band on which is printed "The Simpsons." Flip-up cover over face shows a hologram of Bart. Bagged. . . . .$3-$8.

Homer gold limited edition, 1999. Fossil. Ceramic storage case. Limited edition of 500. Boxed. . . . .$110-$130.

Homer silver limited edition, 1999. Fossil. Stainless steel. Ceramic storage case. Limited edition of 3,000. Boxed. . . . .$80-$100.

Lisa Simpson Puffa Pal asthma inhaler cover, 1996, Oddball. Australia. Fits over Ventolin, Becioforte and Becotide asthma inhalers.

Simpsons checkbook holder, 1992, Deluxe Corp. This holder, as well as Simpsons checks, were discontinued by Deluxe in spring 1998.

1990. JPI. 4½-by-3½-inch portable player with belt clip and headphones. Battery-operated. Carded. . .$20-$40.

Chair, Bart's Rockin' TV Chair, 1990. 24-inch blue plastic with cushion headrest shaped like Bart's head and arm rests shaped like his hands. Boxed. . . . . .$20-$60.

Checkbook holder, 1992. Deluxe Corp. Hot-pink plastic with faces of Simpsons and their dog, Santa's Little Helper. . .$15.

Double stamp set, Lisa, 1989. Ja-Ru. Six rubber-like stampers, two stamp pads and a small booklet called "My book of stamps." Carded. . . . .$3-$8.

Flashlight, Bart, 1990. Happiness Express. 6-inch flashlight with raised figure of Bart along the side. Battery-operated. Carded. . . . .$5-$15.

Inflatable big body surfer, Homer, Marge and Lisa, 1990. Mattel. 50-by-30-inch plastic inflatable that blows up to form a raft-like flotation device. Sealed. . . . .$15-$25.

Bart Simpson nodder, 1997, Custom Accessories Europe. U.K. Bart's head bobs when the base moves.

Other miscellany

Asthma inhaler cover Puffa Pal, Bart, 1996. Oddball. Australia. 3 inches high. Carded. . . . .$5-$10.

Asthma inhaler cover Puffa Pal, Homer, 1996. Oddball. Australia. 3 inches high. Carded. . . .$5-$10.

Asthma inhaler cover Puffa Pal, Lisa, 1996. Oddball. Australia. 3 inches high. Carded. . . . .$5-$10.

Camera and bum bag, Homer and Bart, 1997. The Boots Co. U.K. 4-inch-wide, 35mm flash camera. Includes film, three AAA batteries and "bum bag" carrying case. Boxed. . . . . .$25-$50.

Cassette player, Walk-A-Long, Bart and Lisa,

Simpsons camera and "bum bag" carrying case, 1997, The Boots Co. U.K. 35mm flash camera, approximately 4 inches wide with slightly raised images of Homer and Bart on the front. Roll of color print film included.

Simpsons pacifiers, 1993, Binky. Soother, left, and latex with a "soft, baby-friendly shield."

She couldn't lay a finger on the watch!

In 1990 Simpsons fans got to rot their teeth for a good cause — owning a nifty promotional watch from Butterfinger candy bars.

The watch was part of a mail-in offer advertised in Simpsons Illustrated magazine and elsewhere. "To get your official Simpsons Wrist Watch," the ads instructed, "send 3 Butterfinger candy wrappers (2.1 oz. or larger), $14.99 (check or money order) and the order form below." The ads gave a retail value of $30 for the watch.

The watch is still a cool addition to any Simpsons collection — although not everyone has viewed the promotion so sweetly.

In a story headlined, "All this for a lousy Simpsons watch," Adweek columnist Laurie Petersen wrote in March 1991 about the trouble her magazine's research director had in obtaining the Butterfinger watch she saw advertised on Baby Ruth candy bars.

It seems Roz Moore ordered the watch Oct. 20 for her husband as a gag Christmas present. Although her check was cashed Nov. 7, she didn't get the watch within six to eight weeks, as promised. Moore then wrote four letters and made two phone calls.

Nestle Foods eventually sent her a $1 coupon with a letter saying that due to "very enthusiastic response" the company was temporarily out of Simpsons watches. There was no timetable given for delivery or instructions on how to get a refund.

Petersen noted that such premiums are supposed to promote customers' emotional attachment to a product. Although sales of Butterfinger and Baby Ruth bars did rise 60 percent in the last three months of 1990, Nestle couldn't count on at least one repeat customer, even after her spouse eventually got his Simpsons premium.

Nodder, Bart, 1997. Custom Accessories Europe. U.K. 8-inch-high figure of Bart mooning. Mounts with hook and loop tape in rear-view window of automobile or other places. Bart's head bobs softly with movement of base. Boxed. . . . .$10-$18.

Pacifier, latex, Baby Bart/Maggie, 1993. Binky. Carded. . . . .$1-$5

Pacifier, soother, Baby Bart/Maggie, 1993. Binky. Carded. . . . .$1-$5.

Pencil Sharpener Twirl-ems, Bart with legs crossed, 1990. Noteworthy. Bart inside liquid-filled dome. Bottom has pencil sharpener. Carded. . . .$2-$7.

Ramada Fun Money $5 certificate, 1994. Coupon to go toward saving 50 percent on Simpsons merchandise. No longer valid. . . . .$1.

Sofa buddies, Bart and Homer, 1997. Vivid Imaginations. U.K. 4-inch-long ceramic decoration showing Homer in his underwear on the sofa and Bart next to him on the floor. Boxed. . . .$10-$20.

Bart and Homer Simpson "sofa buddies" statue, 1997, Vivid Imaginations. U.K. Packaging reads: "This item is not suitable or intended as a child's plaything."

Stamper Pak, Simpsons, 1991. Rubber Stampede. 4-inch-wide rubber-like stampers with ink pad. Sealed. . . . .$5-$7.

Stamper Twirl-ems, Bart with legs crossed, 1990. Noteworthy. Bart inside liquid-filled dome. Bottom has stamper of Bart on skateboard. Carded. . . . .$2-$7.

Stamper Twirl-ems, Bart with legs not crossed, 1990. Noteworthy. Bart inside liquid-filled dome. Bottom has stamper of Bart surfing. Carded. . . . .$2-$7.

Stamper Twirl-ems, Bartman, 1990. Noteworthy. Bartman inside liquid-filled dome. Bottom has stamper design of Bartman. Carded. . . . .$2-$7.

Suitcase, "Family Vacation" child-size, 1990. 12-by-19-inch green vinyl with purple trim. Design shows numerous station wagons packed with luggage on top. A circular design on side shows Simpsons. . . . .$25.

Telephone, Bart, 1990. Columbia Tel-Com. 8-inch-high phone shaped like Bart sitting and holding red slingshot. Eyes flash when phone rings. Boxed. . . . .$20-$50.

Bart Simpson Puffa Pal asthma inhaler cover, 1996, Oddball. Australia.

Bart Simpson "Right-on, dude" metal key ring, 1990, Gift Creations.

Homer Simpson Puffa Pal asthma inhaler cover, 1996, Oddball. Australia.

Bart Simpson telephone, 1990, Columbia Tel-Com. 8-inch-high phone with eyes that flash when the phone rings. As a display item and conversation piece, it can't be beaten. But as a phone, it's nothing to call home about. It's awkward to hold and even stranger to use — kind of like talking into a doll's butt.

Simpsons PVC key ring, 1990. Made of hard molded yellow plastic.

Photo index

· ·

To order copies
of this book

To order "Collecting Simpsons! An Unofficial Guide to Merchandise from 'The Simpsons'™" by mail, please send the following:

■ A completed order form (see below).

■ For U.S. residents only, a check or money order for $27.00 for each book, made payable to "KML Enterprises." For residents of other countries, an international money order for $35 for each book in U.S. funds made payable to "KML Enterprises."

These amounts include shipping and applicable sales taxes.

(Sorry, no cash or C.O.D.'s please!)

Address your order to:
KML Enterprises
Box 292
Liverpool, N.Y. 13088

Please allow four to six weeks for delivery

_____

Quick Order Form

(For U.S. orders)
Please send the following book:
_____ copies of Collecting Simpsons! @ $27.00 each $_____

(For international orders)
Please send the following book:
_____ copies of Collecting Simpsons! @ $35.00 each $_____

Total Amount $_____

Book(s) are to be mailed to:

Name:_____

Address:_____

City: _____ State _____ Postal code _____ Country _____

Telephone: _____

E-mail address _____

For bulk orders or other inquiries, write to the above address, or e-mail the author at BartFan@aol.com